Journal of the
Critical Ethnic Studies Association

VOLUME 1 · ISSUE 2
FALL 2015

Guest Editors' Introduction

Racial Comparativism Reconsidered

DANIKA MEDAK-SALTZMAN AND ANTONIO T. TIONGSON JR.

In recent years, the turn to the comparative has become a prominent and defining feature in the study of race and ethnicity, constituting one of the major currents in ethnic studies and becoming the primary mode of analysis in the field. More broadly, comparativeness now serves as the guiding paradigm for ethnic studies scholarship, with much of the contemporary work on race and racialization coming to be informed by a comparative mode of analysis. Accordingly, this intellectual approach has come to be held as a scholarly ideal, considered indispensable to the project of ethnic studies. We see this reflected, over the course of the last two decades, not only in the emphasis on the "comparative" in ethnic studies graduate programs across the nation[1] but also in the growth of publications engaged in comparative work that span multiple disciplinary formations from literature to history.[2] With few exceptions, however, there has yet to be a sustained and critical interrogation of the implications of this shift for the study of race and ethnicity—let alone the development of a set of guiding questions inaugurated by this shift that might help clarify what is gained by engaging in comparativist scholarship.[3] For that matter, it is also not always clear what constitutes comparative scholarship, or if there is strong agreement among race and ethnic studies scholars on the question of what is distinctive about comparative approaches. An examination of this trend reveals that there is nothing inherently enabling or subversive about comparative approaches and models irrespective of the currency and prestige that this kind of work has achieved. In fact, the valorization of comparativeness, which sees such an approach as an unassailable value in and of itself, has helped to obscure that the need to theorize and problematize what it means to engage in comparative scholarship remains largely underexplored.

This special issue constitutes a critical engagement with comparative scholarship and approaches by scrutinizing the challenges and complications that arise out of this kind of work and considers the stakes—theoretical, political, and methodological—raised in the process. Collectively, the pieces in this volume represent a provocation to think through the attendant set of theoretical/political tensions and contradictions inherent in comparative scholarship. The issue is motivated by what Grace Kyungwon Hong and Roderick A. Ferguson have described as "a desire to identify and invent analytics through which to compare racial formations, in distinction to comparative race scholarship that simply parallels instances of historical similarity across racial groups in the United States."[4] Emanating from a variety of disciplinary and theoretical vantage points, these contributions help to elucidate the parameters of critical comparative race studies frameworks by underscoring the following limitations: the notion that particular frameworks and methods will be equally applicable across racialized groups in the United States, the problems inherent in counteracting binary studies of race by replacing them with another binary or assuming a level of equivalence among all binaries, the problems in engaging in comparative critique framed by an investment in cross-racial solidarity, the failure to grapple with how histories of colonialism and their legacies remain present and relevant in Europe and Asia as much as they do in settler colonial North America, and the failure to account for the heterogeneity of race within North American settler colonial contexts and the vexed relationship between Indigenous and diasporic subjects.

INDIGENEITY, AFFECT, AND CONJUNCTURE

A recurrent theme taken up by many of the articles in this issue revolves around how engagement with Native theorizing, Indigeneity, and settler colonial paradigms serves to complicate comparative race scholarship in crucial ways. In centering Indigeneity, this issue draws attention to a subject and theoretical frame that has been increasingly taken up in a variety of disciplines—with varying degrees of success—and considers the nature of this engagement. Danika Medak-Saltzman's article, for example, begins the issue and raises the point that one of the problems of being a new accessory to scholarly endeavors, much as in the fashion industry (tribal prints, anyone?), is that "Indigeneity" is often invoked whether or not one has a nuanced understanding of the particularities of experience, histories, and contemporary struggles that are bound up in the use of the term itself. At the cores of the vast majority of Indigenous epistemes are understandings of reciprocity and responsibility that are inextricable from the material or theoretical. This ought to trouble the fact that the influx in usage of Indigeneity has come to be associated with imbuing one's work with academic cachet but not with an associated sense of responsibility to Indigenous communities or to furthering Indigenous studies scholarship in a meaningful way. Instead, the corresponding responsibility of scholars who engage with Indigeneity to recognize and reckon with the individual and collective complicity of all "arrivants" (whether by choice or by force)[5] in the continued dispossession of Indigenous peoples is usually avoided at all costs. This is, then, a trend that reveals how little those employing Indigeneity actually understand, since it leaves a critical engagement with the continued dispossession of Indigenous peoples as neglected as it would be complicating to notions of race, reparations, decolonization, resurgence, and comparativism in North America.

Put differently, the embrace of Indigeneity is often predicated on disavowals and rejections that serve to circumvent engaging in critical, and potentially fruitful, conversations. These range from seemingly harmless dismissals that ignore to the feverish undermining of Indigenous claims as though they are anti-X (with X being another group who sees discussing Indigeneity as a means of silencing their own experiences—but seems to see no such problem with continuing to silence Indigenous experiences) and to the distortion and misrepresentation of Indigenous studies arguments that are then used as evidence of a lack of intellectual sophistication on the part of Native peoples or Indigenous studies scholars (see the critique that Nandita Sharma and Cynthia Wright offer in response to Bonita Lawrence and Enakshi Dua's article[6]). This reveals a fundamental neglect of the significance of Indigenous difference and a refusal to engage with what this might mean, and why it matters. Whatever means are used to dismiss or gesture toward rather than critically engage the intellectual concerns brought by Indigenous studies scholars, a critical ethnic studies project must take the necessity of such critical engagement seriously if we are to actually incorporate Indigeneity as a lens of analysis in a meaningful and substantive manner. Iyko Day provides such a critical engagement, exploring the idea of a settler colonial binary through a focus on the interplay of Indigeneity and antiblackness/Afro-pessimism in the continental United States. In deexceptionalizing settler colonial critique and Afro-pessimist thought, Day strives to open up lines of inquiry and think through the parameters of settler colonial capitalism as an immanent frame for an analysis of colonial dispossession, racial capitalism, and antiblackness. In his article, George Luna-Peña's analysis goes south of the Mexico-U.S. border in his interrogation of settler colonialism and the erasure of Native presence in the context of the Mexicali Valley. Luna-Peña reconfigures the Mexicali as a settler colonial space, spotlighting how the ideology of *mestizaje* serves to recapitulate the logic of settler colonialism. Like the aforementioned scholars, Antonio T. Tiongson Jr. engages with settler colonial critique through his problematizing of the investments that punctuate Afro-Asian inquiry. Grappling with the challenges and complications of comparative critique, Tiongson takes Afro-Asian inquiry to task for the way it supports settler colonialist logics and assumptions as evidenced, for example, by its conflation of Native peoples with other minoritized groups and its collapsing of the overlapping, yet distinct, processes of racialization and colonization.

Another recurrent theme in this issue is how race and comparativism can be considered vis-à-vis concepts of affect, intimacies, and violence. Medak-Saltzman's article centers on what she describes as the haunted logics of empire as she links Japanese and U.S. settler colonial projects within a transnational imagination. In doing so, she sheds light on how the haunted logics of empire that remain embedded in archives are also reinforced in educational systems and cyclically reproduced and consumed in scholarship about Indigenous peoples—particularly in studies undertaken outside of, or without engaging with, the field of Native American and Indigenous studies. Beverly M. Weber's article takes racial comparative, cultural, and literary analysis to an imagined Europe in her examination of how Yoko Tawada's stories explore, gesture to, and use racial intimacies, and pull on anxieties in the triangulation of relationships—spanning time and space as well as history and fiction—among European, Asian, and African contexts. Weber's contribution is complemented by Medak-Saltzman's theorization of the haunted logics of empire as she links Japanese and U.S. settler colonial projects within a transnational imagination. In both articles, the affective serves as an opening into violent intimacies that undergird processes of racialization and settler colonial endeavors in a wide range of contexts that span North America and Europe with gestures to Africa and Asia writ broadly.

A third theme revolves around what Shu-mei Shih has delineated as "the conjuncture of time and place in each instance of racialization" and what Susan Koshy has described as the "new conjuncture" that necessitates analytics that can grapple with how time and place are co-implicated and mutually constituted as well as speak to the exigencies of the current historical moment.[7] Echoing Stuart Hall's theorization of conjuncture, a number of contributions pay close attention to the need to consider *both* time and place in critical considerations of comparativity.[8] Tiongson's article, for instance, delineates how for a number of race and ethnic studies scholars, comparative work must necessarily be conjunctural, attuned and attentive to historical and political shifts that render a particular moment distinct and necessitate a rethinking of analytics we deploy and the politics we engage in. In her article, Weber focuses on a particular historical conjuncture marked by the intimate encounters among the shifting formations of Africa, Asia, and Europe and the collapsing of time experienced by characters in Tawada's narratives. Luna-Peña delves into another distinct conjuncture characterized by the construction of the Mexicali Valley as a settler colonial space in which the discourse of *mestizaje* serves to uphold the logics of settler colonialism and mediate claims of belonging by Chinese inhabiting this area—claims centering on their deservingness to access and possess Indigenous land.

CONCLUSION

While this special issue takes its place within the growing literature of comparative ethnic studies, it departs from the bulk of this literature in the way it takes a self-reflexive stance, endeavoring to challenge rather than taking as self-evident the normative frames by which comparative work has been understood and conducted. Each contribution suggests an alternative interpretive grid for comparative work, one that is not predicated on a presumption of congruence, symmetry, and commensurability or grounded in finding "commonalities" or "similarities" that could then serve as the basis for interethnic identification and coalition building—as so much comparative scholarship has centered on in the past. In doing so, this issue puts into focus "the limits of the notion of parallel minoritization at the heart of coalition politics."[9] It goes beyond what hitherto has been the sine qua non of comparative ethnic studies scholarship: the evocation and excavation of patterns of similarities and differences—a pattern that we have largely steered away from in this issue as a means of representing alternatives to much of the extant scholarship that has been refracted largely through this lens. Instead, this special issue seeks to elucidate the parameters of a *transnational, intersectional, relational, genealogical,* and *conjunctural* comparative ethnic studies project and proposes analytics that could serve as a productive site for critical ethnic studies scholars to more rigorously and profoundly engage in comparative work. The issue represents an effort to think through the comparative impulse animating the field of ethnic studies at the current moment. It aims to advance an analytic of comparative racial formations, that is, a theoretical frame capable of grappling with what Traise Yamamoto has described as "disparities, disjunctions and incommensurabilities (that) exist between differently racialized groups."[10] In keeping with the journal's mission statement, this volume offers "new analytical languages and paradigms" that serve as a point of departure for mapping "an emergent Critical Ethnic Studies project for the 21st century." In short, the issue represents a timely and needed contribution intended to signal a shift in comparative race scholarship, and by doing so, works to broaden the terrain and terms of this kind of work and place it on a fundamentally different ground—one that reckons head on with the polyvalences of race and the intricate interlacings of racial formations across time and space.

DANIKA MEDAK-SALTZMAN is assistant professor of ethnic studies at the University of Colorado, Boulder, and author of *Specters of Colonialism: Native Peoples, Visual Cultures, and Colonial Projects in the United States and Japan (1860–1904)* (Minnesota, forthcoming).

ANTONIO T. TIONGSON JR. is assistant professor of American studies at the University of New Mexico. He is author of *Filipinos Represent: DJs, Racial Authenticity, and the Hip-hop Nation* (2013) and coeditor of the anthology *Positively No Filipinos Allowed: Building Communities and Discourse* (2006).

NOTES

1. By way of example, the Department of Ethnic Studies at the University of Colorado at Boulder recently launched a Comparative Ethnic Studies PhD program that "offers an innovative and streamlined path to provide students with broad training to enable them to research and analyze the intersectional and relational workings of race, ethnicity, gender, class, and sexuality in national and transnational contexts" (see http://www.colorado.edu/ethnicstudies/grad/phd_program.html), whereas the Department of Ethnic Studies at the University of California, San Diego, describes itself as "an inter-disciplinary social science department specializing in analytic, *comparative,* and theoretical approaches to the study of ethnicity and race" (emphasis ours) (see http://www.ethnicstudies.ucsd.edu/graduate-studies/index.html). Here the CU Boulder description is set apart from the more standard claim to comparativism (reflected in UCSD's statement) by specifying its methods are "intersectional and relational." For further discussion of this issue please see "Afro-Asian Inquiry and the Problematics of Comparative Critique" by Antonio T. Tiongson Jr. in this issue.

2. Included in this body of work are Nicholas De Genova, ed., *Racial Transformations: Latinos and Asians Remaking the United States* (Durham, N.C.: Duke University Press, 2006); Leslie Bow, *Partly Colored: Asian Americans and Racial Anomaly*

in the Segregated South (New York: New York University Press, 2010); Helen Heran Jun, *Race for Citizenship: Black Orientalism and Asian Uplift from Pre-Emancipation to Neoliberal America* (New York: New York University Press, 2011); Lanny Thompson, *Imperial Archipelago: Representation and Rule in the Insular Territories under U.S. Dominion after 1898* (Honolulu: University of Hawai'i Press, 2010); Scott Kurashige, *The Shifting Grounds of Race: Black and Japanese Americans in the Making of Multiethnic Los Angeles* (Princeton, N.J.: Princeton University Press, 2008); Julia H. Lee, *Interracial Encounters: Reciprocal Representations in African and Asian American Literatures, 1896–1937* (New York: New York University Press, 2011); and Tiya Miles and Patricia Holland, eds., *Crossing Waters, Crossing Worlds: The African Diaspora in Indian Country* (Durham, N.C.: Duke University Press, 2006).

3. An exception is Grace Kyungwon Hong and Roderick A. Ferguson, eds., *Strange Affinities: The Gender and Sexual Politics of Comparative Racialization* (Durham, N.C.: Duke University Press, 2011).

4. Hong and Ferguson, *Strange Affinities*, 1.

5. Jodi A. Byrd, *The Transit of Empire: Indigenous Critiques of Colonialism* (Minneapolis: University of Minnesota Press, 2011), 6. "Arrivants" is a term Jodi A. Byrd "borrows from the African Caribbean poet Kamau Braithwaite to signify those people forced into the Americas through the violence of European and Anglo-American colonialism and imperialism around the globe" (xix).

6. Nandita Sharma and Cynthia Wright, "Decolonizing Resistance, Challenging Colonial States," *Social Justice* 35, no. 3 (2008/2009): 120–38; Bonita Lawrence and Enakshi Dua, "Decolonizing Antiracism," *Social Justice* 32, no. 4 (2005): 120–43.

7. Shu-mei Shih, "Comparative Racialization: An Introduction," *PMLA* 123, no. 5 (October 2008): 1349; Susan Koshy, "Why the Humanities Matter for Race Studies Today," *PMLA* 123, no. 5 (October 2008): 1546, 1547. This is a phrase Koshy uses several times in her article.

8. See Stuart Hall, "New Ethnicities," in *Black British Cultural Studies: A Reader*, ed. Houston A. Baker, Manthia Diawara, and Ruth H. Lindeborg (Chicago: University of Chicago Press, 1996), 163–72. See also Stuart Hall, "What Is This 'Black' in Black Popular Culture," in *Black Popular Culture*, ed. Michelle Wallace and Gina Dent (Seattle: Bay Press, 1992), 21–33.

9. Colleen Lye, "The Afro-Asian Analogy," *PMLA* 123, no. 5 (October 2008): 1734.

10. Traise Yamamoto, "An Apology to Althea Connor: Private Memory, Public Racialization, and Making a Language," *Journal of Asian American Studies* 2, no. 3 (February 2002): 24.

ESSAYS

Empire's Haunted Logics

Comparative Colonialisms and the Challenges of Incorporating Indigeneity

DANIKA MEDAK-SALTZMAN

> Indigenous peoples in Atlantic and Pacific new world geographies remain colonized as an ongoing lived experience that is not commensurable with the stories the postcolonial pluralistic multiculture wants to tell of itself.
>
> —Jodi A. Byrd, *The Transit of Empire*

In no uncertain terms, Indigenous populations remain entrenched in fundamentally different situations than those faced by other racialized groups. Although the truth of it is inconvenient and unpalatable, the reality that settler colonialism—which Patrick Wolfe tells us is a process rather than an event[1]—is ongoing makes it all the more conspicuous that the function and effects of settler colonialism remain largely unseen by those who benefit from them. Yet, as incisive as Jodi A. Byrd's observation is, we must also recognize that the resistance to and failure to see Indigeneity, or the critical contexts central to understanding Indigenous peoples' historical and contemporary experiences, is decidedly not limited to thinking from "new world geographies" nor to those who insist that our world is a "postcolonial pluralistic multiculture."[2] For these reasons, one might expect that the recent and increasingly common invocation of the term *Indigeneity* in cross-disciplinary and interdisciplinary scholarly production would be a movement immediately welcomed by Indigenous studies scholars. However, inasmuch as such references to "Indigeneity" may be intended to help finally account for and draw attention to the way academics contribute to the pervasive vanishing and diminishment of Native presence, significance, and realities, these mentions remain largely, and troublingly, cursory. The invocation of Indigeneity across disciplines cannot yet be counted on as an indication of an author's fluency with the legal, epistemological, and political particularities of Native peoples' experiences with settler colonial realities—

which one might reasonably otherwise expect from scholarly engagement with intellectual subjects. Instead, this trend seems to be the most recent example of a familiar, and superficial, pattern of (non)engagement with Native peoples, histories, and Indigenous studies scholarship in settler colonial societies writ large. "Indigeneity" is all too often invoked as a term—rather than a concept—which reduces it to jargon, removes it from its vital context, and embeds it in writing that otherwise betrays a very limited intellectual and scholarly understanding of Native experiences, issues, and histories. This is to say (to borrow from Emma Perez's *Decolonial Imaginary*[3]) that Indigeneity is often invoked in a manner that renders it as merely an "appendage" to the real stories, which is markedly different from engaging it as a subject with its own goals. One can make arguments about why this has been the case: perceived paucity of sources (with its emphasis on a very specific and elite colonial print archive), lamentations and assumptions that "we will never know" (which justify not looking for what is there), and the difficulty of combatting the already entrenched Indigenous absence in existing scholarship, among other oft-cited reasons. But such excuses normalize how power is exercised in the production of knowledge and how colonial ideologies have become enmeshed in certain (haunted) ways of thinking about the world.

This tendency cannot be blamed on the perceived "newness" of such interventions, for the practice and discipline of Indigenous studies has been building globally since the 1960s. To be clear, the argument here is not that everyone can or should become Indigenous studies experts.[4] However, we would do well to recognize that when invocations of "Indigeneity" do not anticipate a complicated engagement with Native studies scholarship—even though the field represents half a century of scholarly engagement, theoretical interventions, and actual practice of Indigenous studies—it becomes difficult to see such usage as anything more than self-serving. As long as the superficial invocation of "Indigeneity" is intended to showcase that a scholar has kept up with scholarly trends in the field, rather than an attempt to critically engage with or further Indigenous studies scholarship in a meaningful way, then this tendency ought to be viewed as what it is: a twenty-first-century intellectual example of the time-honored Western tradition of pilfering (lands, resources, ideas, knowledge, theoretical frames, artistic traditions, etc.) from Native peoples for the benefit of the self/nation, with utter disregard to any resulting consequences borne by Indigenous peoples.

Yet how are we to engage with Indigeneity in a substantive manner when it has been sidelined or given cursory treatment in ethnic studies, in many cases as often as it has been in other disciplines? For examples of this, we need look no further than ethnic studies, American studies, or race studies programs that do not include American Indian/Native American/Indigenous studies as part of their curriculum in any significant way. In doing so, instead of framing and engaging Indigenous studies, Indigenous experience, and Indigeneity as *foundational* and *essential* to critical examinations of North American experience, history, and racialization processes, the significance of Indigeneity has instead been undermined and relegated to the realm of the inconsequential: a prehistory or background to the real stories, relegated to the first/last week of class (or to Native history month), and absent from discussions of the civil rights era and contemporary sociopolitical protests in North America, to name but a few examples. A critical ethnic studies must do better than simply adding "and Indians/Native peoples/Indigeneity" to their teaching or writing as a means of performing inclusivity.

There are untold ways that a rigorous incorporation of Indigeneity and Indigenous studies scholarship can strengthen critical ethnic studies and cognate fields, and nuance existing scholarly understandings and conversations by insisting that long-held unquestioned assumptions be reevaluated: as an example, what does it mean to consider the Sand Creek Massacre and the Civil War as different strategic arms reaching toward the same national and economic goals,[5] or to complicate narratives about slavery in North America by recognizing that not only did some Native communities participate in enslaving African peoples, but Native American peoples had also been enslaved and sold across the Atlantic and elsewhere?[6] Critical intellectual engagement with Indigeneity is not about asserting a front-runner status in an "oppression Olympics"—a framing that often serves to silence the concerns of all other groups by asserting one group's experience was the worst of all—rather, it is to acknowledge that including Indigeneity in inter- and transdisciplinary scholarship and collaborations can help us move closer to and beyond the stated objectives of a critical ethnic studies.[7] Setsu Shigematsu and Keith Camacho explain the inherent value in strengthening and undertaking inter- and transdisciplinary scholarship when they write that it "can generate potentially transformative methodologies of knowledge production."[8]

To underscore how engaging Indigeneity in a more complex manner is vital to the success and development of critical ethnic studies in particular and to comparative scholarship more broadly, this article first draws attention to how theories and methods with useful applications in the examination of the experiences of other racialized peoples often fails to achieve the same result when applied indiscriminately to Indigenous contexts. To underscore this, I engage with two familiar concepts—postcolonial haunting and conventions of periodization—to highlight how and why these frames must be reconfigured, or challenged and expanded, if they are to actually incorporate Indigenous peoples and experiences. I also offer one such re-visioning by presenting a new theory of haunting—one more applicable to Indigenous experience—as a step toward the development of new theoretical lenses that critical ethnic and Indigenous studies must continue to cultivate in order to foster an engagement with the unique situations of Indigenous peoples, separately and in concert with the experiences of other racialized groups in North America. Opening such theoretical spaces may allow us to commit ourselves to expanding our thinking beyond the artifice and imposition of disciplinary boundaries, rid our work of problematic suppositions about Native peoples, and challenge ourselves to examine how easily we can, and do, vanish Indigeneity in our scholarship. Further, and as an exercise in working toward and delineating what these "transformative methodologies" might look like, I then offer a reading of an 1860s U.S. political cartoon—which on the surface seems to have little, if anything, to do with Indigeneity, especially since it references Japan's inaugural visit to the United States—to help underscore what becomes visible when images and ideas are reevaluated and freed from the haunted logics of empire.

ON HAUNTOLOGY AND PERIODIZATION

Theories of postcolonial haunting and the trace—although recuperative and valuable to analyzing the experiences and complexities of histories faced by other minoritized groups in North America—provide a perfect example of how the application and utility of popular theoretical frames for examining the experiences of marginalized groups, even in a strictly U.S. context, often does not work when simply extended to the situations faced by Indigenous populations. We cannot simply expect that theoretical frames that are useful in making sense of the experiences of other racialized groups will be equally relevant when applied to Indigenous peoples and contexts. Surely there are cases where this wholesale application works, but it is far more common to see such "inclusion" of Indigeneity as more of an attempt to fit an Indigenous round peg into an all-other-racialized-groups square hole, while avoiding actual engagement with how and why the Indigenous case complicates such theoretical frames. However, the desire to "make" a given theoretical frame "fit" rather than to engage with Indigeneity and all of its attendant complexities represents a settler colonial desire that functions to render the value of, and need for, complex engagement with Indigenous difference inconsequential and irrelevant. This is a line of thinking that relies on the false assumption that Native peoples are simply another minority group in North America—a belief that is not only inaccurate but also serves to blind non-Native peoples to how their presence (even as minoritized groups) on stolen Indigenous territories makes a delicate and complex engagement with questions about collective complicity in the continued dispossession of Indigenous peoples necessary. For this is a complicity that a reckoning with the very fact of that theft, and working toward manifesting the decolonial goals outlined by Indigenous communities and our allies, might go a long way toward addressing.

It seems that due, at least in part, to the general recognition of the shameful history of slavery in the United States—a basic level of visibility denied to Native peoples—it has become possible for scholars, historians, and novelists, among others, to employ ghosts and haunting as theoretically compelling and socially empowering tools for historical examination. From Ralph Ellison's illustration of how that which is hypervisible is also an invisible ghostly presence in *Invisible Man* to Toni Morrison's haunted Sethe, who comes face-to-face with the ghost of the daughter she murdered to save her from slavery, this trope is used far beyond these celebrated literary examples, both within and far afield from African American studies. Yet the very nature of haunting has been useful precisely because, as Avery Gordon tells us, "to be haunted is to be tied to historical and social effects,"[9] even when, or perhaps especially when, these social effects of the past are dismissed as irrelevant and ahistorical or attributed to bitterness that ought to be "gotten over." Indeed, the notion of haunting, often appearing as immutable "traces," has proven a useful device for many groups in North America as they have sought to reveal long-hidden and silenced histories. However, wholesale applications of postcolonial and cultural studies notions of haunting and the trace to the specificity of Native American and Indigenous peoples' experiences presents a distinct problem: precisely because the "fact" of Native vanishing has become part of a "common-sense" belief that renders Indigenous peoples always already ghostly presences, postcolonial notions of haunting and the trace simply cannot serve as recuperative, or decolonial, strategies for Indigenous peoples. Instead, indiscriminate application of these theories to Indigenous contexts manages to reinforce, rather than dismantle, settler colonial logics that mandate, carry out, and insist upon Indigenous absence.

Indian ghosts have been and remain an indelible trope in North American narratives and national mythologies: we see Indigenous "absence" taught in schools, supported by media, and reinforced by statistics that encourage seeing Native peoples and contexts as unworthy of inclusion in studies because our populations are so small. Blaming this absence, neglect, and perceived statistical inconsequence on our small numbers—instead of recognizing the significance of teaching about, reporting on, and including populations that have been intentionally reduced to single-digit percentages of national populations (on our own lands)—shifts responsibility for this continued ignorance away from those who have benefited from settler colonialism and onto the shoulders of the victims and survivors of great violence and invasion. This orchestrated absence and insisted-upon irrelevance is also often unquestioningly reproduced in scholarship—even when the scholarly subject at hand seems to otherwise have little to nothing to do with Indigenous subjects. This pervasive, public, scholarly, and media supported and encouraged manner of thinking about—or more tellingly *not* thinking about—Native peoples is part of the unseen fabric that binds settler colonial societies together, legitimating the presence of all non-Native peoples on stolen land, whether they arrived by choice or by force. For these reasons, any attempt to simply extend notions of postcolonial haunting to Native peoples is neither empowering nor generative; instead, it further entrenches settler colonial fantasies of Indigenous absence that operate to absolve non-Native peoples, living on stolen Native lands, of this original sin.

Therefore, in order to conceive of a theoretically compelling concept of haunting that can better illuminate Indigenous experiences, we must invert the familiar directionality of postcolonial haunting that locates the source of ghostly agency as emanating from the experiential realities of racialized subjects and situates haunting as a consequence of these complicated histories. Indeed, for any theory of haunting to be useful to Indigenous and allied efforts toward decolonization, Indigenous ghosts simply cannot be conceived of as the source of this haunting. Instead, the ghosts that emerge from and haunt settler colonial contexts radiate from their roots in the moral, intellectual, and legal logics developed to legitimate, as necessity, the great violence of empire. Settler colonial societies are haunted by the need to keep these unpalatable truths and their human consequences hidden. This is a feat the ghosts I am describing accomplish by maintaining and reinforcing foundational "truths" and assumptions (e.g., patently false beliefs that Native peoples had no sophisticated forms of governance before the arrival of Europeans) that aid in determining whether, and how, Indigeneity is considered, if it is considered at all. Rendered another way, the logics of empire that haunt settler colonial societies are vestiges of the goals and spirit of colonialism that haunt in order to maintain the foundational narratives of Indigenous absence/inconsequence that justify settler colonial presence on Indigenous lands and manage to absolve guilty consciences in the process. I call these the "specters of colonialism," and they are as pervasive as they are relentless as they work continually and nearly imperceptibly in their efforts to keep the violence, theft, and logics used to legitimate colonial endeavors neatly hidden from view.

Naming these haunted logics the specters of colonialism—a turn of phrase that conjures certain European ghosts of its own—as I call attention to the need to focus on, implement, and contribute to critical Indigenous and ethnic studies theory might seem an odd choice. But this continental intellectual genealogy offers a significant and worthwhile means of considering ghostliness and the nature of haunting and their application to Indigenous contexts. Rather than thinking of that which haunts as alternatively tangible, visible, or as spirits that can be sensed but not seen as they affect the living in a variety of ways, there is a less common, but more theoretically compelling, manner of thinking about haunting that can better lend itself to considerations of Indigenous experiences. That is, when what that which haunts is the very spirit of an idea: Karl Marx and Friedrich Engels's claim that a "specter of communism" was haunting Europe and Jacques Derrida's discussions of the "specters of Marx" are prime examples of this kind of haunting.[10] Adding to the challenges that arise when undertaking academic investigations of that which is both there-and-not-there is the fact that it is often difficult, and at times nearly impossible, to draw attention to that which haunts entire societies. This is precisely the point that Derrida is making regarding the specters of Marx when he coins the term *hauntology*; for the term itself in the original French is a homonym for ontology, literally replacing the study of existence with the study of that which does not exist yet wields considerable influence. These ghostly presences are deep seated and lingering, and they leave indelible traces of themselves that can be read—if we manage to free ourselves from the influence of these specters of colonialism, by learning to see them and resist their influence—to reveal seldom-considered perspectives on the past and present. While Marx and Engels reference ghosts of communism and Derrida the spirit of Marx and the Marxist inheritance, I assert that the specter haunting our world is our colonial inheritance made manifest. I locate the agents, ideologies, practices, and long-lasting effects of colonialism as the sites from which these myriad hauntings emerge, and contend that we are all more influenced by them than we are likely aware. After all, as the specters of colonialism exert their influence in carrying out the goals of the spirit of colonialism, they hold sway over the weight with which Indigeneity and Indigenous concerns are respected, engaged with, and investigated at the same time that they encourage the dismissal of certain questions and the blind acceptance of settler colonial foundational logics. In this way, the specters of colonialism help to justify and promote the very pattern of non-engagement with Indigenous intellectual traditions and Indigenous studies scholarship that this article seeks to trouble.

STATISTICAL IRRELEVANCE, THE ARTIFICE OF BOUNDED TIME, AND COLONIAL OPTICS

There are two key examples of the normalized ways that Native peoples are excluded from scholarship, even in critical ethnic studies, that might serve as a starting point in any endeavor to disrupt the haunted logics of empire. The first is the level of legitimacy given to claims that Native populations are so small that we are "statistically irrelevant" often offered up to explain away or justify why one has neglected (or refused) to include Native peoples in their data and analysis. Yes, we are a very small population on our own lands, thanks to the violence of settler colonialism, but erasure, by any other name, or means, or justification, is still erasure. The second example can begin to be tackled by reframing and reconfiguring how we conceptualize traditional fields and historical periods, what they mean, and why this matters. For embedded within standardized understandings of historical periods are assumptions about the past that the specters of colonialism are invested in maintaining, and these are precisely the assumptions that a critical ethnic studies ought to be invested in disrupting. For example, thanks to the way that academic disciplines have been siloed and how time has been demarcated into specific and bounded historical periods, the specters of colonialism have been able to render the fact and consequences of settler colonialism invisible by making it arduous to work across disciplinary and temporal boundaries in attempts to call attention to subjects other than those privileged by conventional periodization. Here, I shift attention to my larger work examining the relationships between the United States and Japan and the intertwining of their settler colonial projects in the 1870s as an example of how periodization can function to determine which lines of inquiry are considered historically possible. This point of inquiry immediately complicates the way that scholars have long marked the Japanese colonial period as beginning with Japan's takeover of Taiwan in 1895, and simultaneously suggests that Japan was engaging in its own settler colonial projects—two claims considered controversial in Japanese studies. A cemented 1895 "start date" for the Japanese colonial period makes it nearly impossible to argue that Japanese colonialism occurred prior to this, despite the fact that there is ample evidence that Japan's takeover of Indigenous peoples' territories—Ainu lands in the north and Ryūkyū lands in the south—was indeed a settler colonial endeavor being undertaken well before Japan asserted authority over Taiwan, and the Indigenous populations therein. Yet use of this periodization and acceptance of its attendant haunted implications remains common in Japanese studies and history, as does the trend of referring to Japan's takeover of Ainu territories, in particular, as an exercise of "domestic development," even as some in the discipline question both this language usage and the limits imposed by hard and fast notions of historical periods.[11] Although attempts have been made to dismiss these concerns as "semantics," we would do well to recognize how resistance to renaming national activities "colonial" or "settler colonial" (to be more accurate) and questioning or rebounding given time periods (to make visible the significant events that take place across conventional historical periods) are themselves products and evidence of the influence levied by the specters of colonialism.

Similar concerns exist regarding the legitimacy of disciplines beyond Japanese studies, such as Indigenous studies or anthropology, having purview over Ainu subjects. One point of contention for those who want to stake a proprietary claim to Ainu subjects has to do with concerns about Japanese language proficiency. To be sure, it has been, and remains, vital that those engaged in the production of knowledge about Japanese studies subject areas, including Ainu subjects, engage Japanese-language source materials and scholarship proficiently. To these ends, scholars within Japanese studies have taken responsibility for academic gatekeeping, as a matter of principle and intellectual integrity. This vigilance, however, only serves to make it more remarkable that many of these same scholars engage in studies of Ainu subjects without any working level of fluency in Indigenous studies scholarship, which would unquestionably help nuance and inform their scholarship in critical ways. This practice means that even the best-intentioned scholars often end up producing work that is interventionist in their own discipline by beginning conversations that Indigenous studies has had resolved for decades. Native American and Indigenous studies (NAIS), as the field is increasingly known, is a rigorous endeavor that incorporates a vast array of traditional disciplinary vantage points and areas of inquiry, and is understood to have unique goals outside of narrowly focused investigations of Native relationships with settler colonial nation states. However, *the same cannot yet be said* for the Ainu case, and so long as investigating Ainu subjects remains the domain of a Japanese studies that is not in conversation with NAIS, it may be tethered to and limited by this constraint for some time to come. It is this chasm—existing among those working *on* Indigenous peoples (in other disciplines), those striving to simply *include* "and Indigeneity" (to broaden their perceived comparative scope, sans nuanced engagement), and those working *in* Indigenous studies—that must be overcome if we aim to produce scholarship that is no longer haunted by the goals, assumptions, and logics of empire.

To illustrate this, I now turn to an image from 1860 that foregrounds a peculiar organizing optics of colonialism, a visual regime that is similar to those that arise across incidences marked by empire and power imbalances. These colonial optics organize how, if, and for what purpose Indigeneity is seen. Examined with this in mind, the weight of Native presence on lands coveted for U.S. and Japanese nation-building projects of the mid-nineteenth century becomes more readily evident, whether the Indigenous figure is deployed or obscured as these expansionist national projects are carried out, envisioned, and depicted. Seeing hypervisibility and invisibility as being opposite sides of the same coin frequently spent in the service of systems of domination is a strategy I borrow from black cultural studies. As Nicole R. Fleetwood claims in *Troubling Vision,* if *visibility* "implies a state of being able to be seen," then, by logical extension, *invisibility* implies a state of *not* being able to be seen.[12] Hypervisibility, however, does not simply mean ever-present visibility. Rather, the concept of *hypervisibility* has been developed as an interventionist term for describing the overproduction of visual material that portrays Others in manners that have been so overdetermined and so ever-present that they become of little consequence, thereby rendering that which is hypervisible nearly, or effectively, invisible. Put another way, the overrepresentation of an Othered group can either, or simultaneously, represent, reproduce, and further entrench social and political invisibility for particular populations, effectively disappearing these groups almost entirely from the landscape of hegemonic discourse. Approached this way then, even an image that does not overtly represent Indigenous peoples can be read in a manner that exposes how this same image erases Indigenous experiences of, and existence during, these same historical moments. Thus, in order to tease out Indigeneity and Indigenous experiences from the tangled strands of intertwined histories, we must not only recognize the way that the haunted logics of empire are working to prevent us from doing so, but—and even if we have only been exposed to thinking that focuses on how the colonizers influence the colonized—we must also honor that historical influences levied on local and global events have always run both ways and ought to have disciplinary implications.

OUR VISITORS

On June 2, 1860, a political cartoon titled "Our Visitors" appeared in *Harper's Weekly: A Journal of Civilization,* a popular news, political, and literary magazine first published in 1857. At the same time that *Harper's Weekly* provided news about local, national, and international happenings for its readers, the publication's stories and images often introduced and reinforced commonly held U.S. beliefs about cultural others by intimately and often visually intertwining race-based ideologies with national fantasies of a uniquely American divine providence. The ubiquity of such images during this publication's formative years, and across the news media of the time, played integral roles in carrying out the operations of empire and in justifying and legitimizing settler colonial nation-building projects. With this in mind, my close reading of "Our Visitors" is aimed at considering what the image was crafted to convey to its intended 1860s audience, alongside what a twenty-first-century vantage point makes visible regarding the future that this image anticipates. Moreover, this reading is offered as an example of how we can begin to call the haunted logics of empire into question, recognize the power in seeing the unseen, and begin to free ourselves, and the scholarship we produce, from the influence of the specters of colonialism.

"Our Visitors" presents the viewer with two contrasting figures, one comfortably seated in his own home and positioned slightly right of center, and the other, a visitor to this home who is entering from the left. The text below the image identifies the home's occupant as Brother Jonathan, an early version of the character who would become Uncle Sam, and one an 1860s audience would have been able to recognize even without his usual stovepipe hat, given his standard attire: striped pants and a black coat worn over a vest covered in stars. The other man is a be-slippered, sword-carrying, dark-complected man, entering Jonathan's home from the left, and carrying an unlit candle in a holder upon which "Japan" is written. This guiding text on the candleholder is reinforced by the text below the image that identifies

"Our Visitors," *Harper's Weekly: A Journal of Civilization* (June 2, 1860): 352.
Courtesy HarpWeek.

this man simply as a "Japanese Visitor." Naming him this way, instead of simply relying on the character's clothing (kimono, obi, and hakama) and hairstyle, ensured that the audience, who were only just becoming acquainted with the visual cues of "Japaneseness," recognized this man as representing the nation of Japan. *Harper's* audience was familiar with political cartoons using particular characters to portray specific nations (such as Brother Jonathan, and his British counterpart John Bull), and by 1860, its readers were also well aware of the visual signifiers of racial difference that had already become fixed in media portrayals of black, Chinese, Native, Irish, and other others who were often portrayed in political cartoons. After more than two hundred years of restricting travel to, trade with, and diplomatic relations with Western countries, Japan "opened," first, to the United States in the 1850s.[13] For this reason, representations of Japaneseness were still unfamiliar to U.S. audiences. However, the arrival of the inaugural Japanese Embassy in 1860 made it vital for the media to document and comment on the arrival and experiences of these Japanese visitors, thus artists often relied on elements and signifiers usually associated with other races. In this case, we can see this in the artist's rendering of footwear (slippers rather than geta) and the overly pronounced angular shape of the eyes as well as in the man's darkened skin tone and the fullness of his lips—familiar markers of Chineseness and blackness, respectively. The clothing, body language, and markers of race and nationality that the characters display work to visually manifest existing 1860s ideas about race, racial hierarchy, and narratives of national uniqueness central to a reading of this image.

The entire scene depicted in "Our Visitors" is set in the heart of an 1860s U.S. living room replete with hallmarks of modernity and success, the centerpiece of which is a lamp labeled "civilization." To the right of this literal and figurative center, we see Jonathan, who only moments before had been in the midst of reading an issue of *Harper's Weekly*. In stark contrast with how comfortable Jonathan seems, surrounded by the hallmarks of civilization, the Japanese man is portrayed as if he is emerging from darkness as he enters the room and extends his candle toward the "light of civilization." Jonathan looks up from his paper to see this visitor entering the room and looking intently at Jonathan. In response, and with one eyebrow raised inquisitively, Jonathan looks at his visitor and says, "Ah! And, pray, what can I do for you?" Jonathan's wry smile, as he makes this inquiry, suggests that he already has an inkling regarding what might be of interest to his visitor. This reading of Jonathan's expression as he queries his visitor is reinforced by the conspicuousness of Japan's unlit candle being extended toward the light of civilization for lighting. Moreover, this suggestion that Japan might need the United States to "do" this for them is also reflective of popular perceptions of Japan, which were rooted in part in U.S. officials' descriptions of Japan as a "semi-barbarous" nation, and thus in need of assistance in modernizing. In response to this, the Japanese visitor says, "If you please, I would like to borrow a little of your light." In this way, the image frames the United States and its citizens (represented by Jonathan) as bearers, brokers, and beneficiaries of civilization, while Japan is rendered as merely interested in being supplied with these skills.

"Our Visitors" mirrors the anxieties and excitement that had been building among the populace since President Millard Fillmore sent a U.S. fleet led by Commodore Matthew Perry that departed in 1852 intending to "open" Japan—a feat other Western nations had previously attempted, to no avail. The "visitor" that this image represents was the first official Japanese visit to a Western nation since Perry's success inaugurating U.S.-Japan relations. Many saw Japan's decision to send an embassy to the United States, before sending one to other Western nations, as a coup—attributable to the divine providence and manifest destiny of the United States—despite the matter of geographic proximity and Japan's goal of quickly learning about the West that surely held sway over Japan's decision.

Evidence of the United States' belief in its own manifest destiny can be seen in the fixtures around the room that represent the era's national social, economic, racial, and technological progress. To draw attention to the relationship between the light of civilization at the image's center and the gas chandelier, the artist provides a visual link, a gas line, that extends between them indicating that it is the same civilizing fuel that makes it possible to illuminate this room and the cultural and material signifiers of progress in the room. Rather than relying on the audience's ability to infer from the image that this shared power source represents an important linkage, the artist affixes each light with guiding text—the lamp with "civilization," and the shades inscribed "literature," "art," and "commerce"—that works in concert with the illustration to link technological advances with these civilized, and civilizing, arts. References to literature, art, and commerce—the very hallmarks of civilization—are evident throughout the room. Literature, and by extension literateness, for example, are represented in two ways in "Our Visitors." The first is in the fact that Jonathan is reading an issue of *Harper's Weekly,* a detail that links Jonathan (representing the United States) and the *Harper's* readers together as they simultaneously participate in literate (and therefore civilized) society. This mirroring encourages the readers to see themselves reflected in this image and thus as a part of the larger whole (U.S. civilized society) that Jonathan represents. In this way, the image reflects back at the readers that they too, in reading *Harper's Weekly,* are in the midst of using a specific "civilized" skill that binds them to an imagined collective of other nineteenth-century *Harper's Weekly* readers.

As Benedict Anderson argues in *Imagined Communities,* print capitalism, the printing press, and the resulting ability to distribute reading and visual material to people across significant distances provided individuals with the opportunity to cultivate a sense of self as part of a larger (national) whole.[14] As Anderson explains, imagined communities are comprised of people who, it can be assumed, will never meet yet who hold certain values, histories, and approaches to life, collectively, in common. Moreover, Anderson argues that the development and proliferation of broadly configured socially imagined communities played an essential role in larger projects of nation-building and nation-state formation in Europe, Asia, and the Middle East.

While *Imagined Communities* is considered foundational scholarship that has been valuable across many disciplines—and is particularly useful in examining this aspect of "Our Visitors"—the fact that Anderson's articulation of imagined community formation is predicated on, and intimately linked to, the written word and the printing press has led some to approach it with suspicion. After all, Anderson's privileging of the printed word, over other equally significant and reliable manners of documentation—an assertion that insists that the presence of certain products of the (Western) industrial revolution were vital precursors to the development of imagined communities and the concept of nation—is deeply problematic. Such an assertion implicitly indicts many non-Western communities, and those whose documentation of history and narrative have long taken place in forms that are not "written"—in the sense Anderson implies—as being, therefore, unable, if not culturally or intellectually incapable, of forming nations of imagined communities. That Anderson's work is embedded with biases and myopia rooted in "civ/sav"[15] binary logics makes using it without challenging this bias questionable, particularly when Anderson is being referenced in an essay that examines how the specters of colonialism continue to haunt academic production and consumption. To my mind, using Anderson without considering and acknowledging the implicit and deeply rooted biases that his work reinforces—unintentionally perhaps, but nevertheless—is one of the many ways that the specters of colonialism continue as active presences in contemporary scholarship. That being said, the tableau presented in "Our Visitors" was indeed made widely available thanks to the printing press, and Jonathan's mirroring of *Harper's* readers serves to strengthen the viewer's sense of belonging to the specific imagined community that Jonathan represents.

Under the lamp and bathed in the light of civilization lays the second reference to the written word, perhaps even The Word. Although it is difficult to discern in the original, and even more so once reduced for publication here, the letters *I-B-L-E* are just barely visible along the spine of this book. Although we cannot know whether the original audience had difficulty making out the title of this book, the inclusion of the Bible, and therefore Christianity, in this tableau does more than mark both the home (read as the civilized world) and Brother Jonathan (read as the United States) as Christian. The placement of the Bible at the center of the scene also invites a contemporary audience to weigh the role and complicity of Christianity in the violence and spread of empire in the name of "civilization."

Indeed, by the time of the European "Age of Discovery," a euphemistic term that describes a period marked by unprecedented theft, slaughter, and subjugation of non-Christian peoples and lands, Christianity had already long been used to justify actions that were antithetical to the principles of the faith. There are three papal bulls from this period that dictated the rules of the age and lent an air of righteousness to claims that all Christians were civilized and all non-Christians were savage.[16] These documents declared that the lands, resources, bodies, and labor of non-Christian peoples (that had not already been "discovered" and claimed by another Christian nation) could be claimed, by "Right of Discovery," for the Christian nation "discovering" it; these religious proclamations further specified that, according to what would be called the Law of Nations, lands already claimed by one Christian nation could not be claimed by another Christian nation. A fact little known outside of Native studies is that this same "right of discovery" was written into U.S. law in 1823 by Chief Justice John Marshall in *Johnson v. M'Intosh,* the first in the trilogy of laws that remain the foundation of Federal Indian Law. In opposition with the U.S. goal to preserve the separation of Church and State, Federal Indian Law and the U.S. Supreme Court still rely on the intimate intertwining of Christian doctrine and jurisprudence codified as precedent by Marshall, who sought to justify European claims to North American lands while still recognizing (and limiting) American Indian sovereignty and did so by ultimately declaring Native tribes "domestic dependent nations." Importantly, the fact that the mores of Christianity and the violent actions undertaken in the name of civilization were fundamentally at odds was not lost on Native peoples; treaty commissioners, Indian agents, and others often commented on this "troubling" fact, even asking to be replaced since they had lost any moral credibility with the tribes as a result. But confronting the illogical and unjust behavior undertaken in the name of Christianity and its civilizing mission did little, in most cases, to slow the dispossession, colonization, death, and forced assimilation inflicted on Native peoples by the newcomers.

By inscribing "literature" and "art" on separate chandelier shades, the image encourages a reader to consider these discrete elements of civilized cultural production and to see how art is represented around the room. Ranging from the detail and design of the artistic metal work on the lamp and chandelier to the more obvious framed paintings on the walls, art is also represented in several ways in this room. The presence of these decorative elements, already imbued with weight by the guiding text that marks art as important, lend themselves to a reading that sees the attainment of civilization and the spoils acquired in conquest as part and parcel of developing both an appreciation for art and the accumulation of wealth necessary for art acquisition.

Facing the viewer and partially obscured by the smoke from Brother Jonathan's cigar is a painting of a large, seafaring vessel. It is unclear whether this painting was intended to conjure a particular voyage, a famous ship, or a particular moment in history in the minds of the audience. What we do know is that by including a painted ship as a part of this tableau, intended to mark the United States as a home of Western civilization, the artist demonstrated how ships were vital to U.S. commerce and economy in 1860 in a general sense, and this image also likely reminded readers in particular of the groundbreaking trips that Commodore Perry took to Japan in 1853–54. Whether the intended audience saw Perry's success or a gesture to maritime economic endeavors in the painting behind Brother Jonathan's head, the painted ship is not the only way "commerce" is represented in the room. A miniature steam locomotive sits atop the mantel on the far right of the room, reminding the 1860s audience that the railroad made it increasingly possible to spread progress westward and travel great distances at ever-increasing rates. Although completion of the transcontinental railroad would not occur for nearly another decade, the desire to have the railroad link the United States from sea to shining sea was already a familiar national goal. At this time, most major cities in the northern and midwestern states were connected by rail, and it was not uncommon for people and news reports alike to mention all that the railway had made possible, and to imagine what a transcontinental railway might bring in the future. Thus, the model train above the fireplace reminded the reader about the ingenuity, industry, modernity, and general character of the nation. However, we must remember that pervasive narratives of the American West and the spread of railways that focus on the technologies or the racialized labor that made such expansion possible yet fail to incorporate the experiences of Indigenous peoples and their extensive resistance efforts are always already haunted by the specters of colonialism.

Of course the creator of "Our Visitors" could not have known how future events would unfold, but by capturing a particular logic of empire that sees the United States as the beating heart of civilization charged with carrying this light outward to illuminate the darkest corners of the savage world. This image represents nineteenth-century narratives, rooted in the linearity of progress that fixes whole peoples as either the purveyors or victims of civilizing endeavors. It is precisely these binary logics that cement understandings of the directionality of influence as flowing only from colonizer to colonized, a framing that Indigenous studies aims to complicate. For example, when the verbal exchange between Jonathan and the Japanese visitor is considered from an Indigenous studies vantage point, one sees in the visitor's request, "to borrow a little" of Jonathan's "light," more than a passing reference to the information-gathering elements of Japan's early missions to the States. To be sure, the 1860s embassy and the Iwakura mission that followed, in 1871, sought to learn from and about the Western world, but the overdetermined flow of influence and the artifice of conventional historical periodization virtually prescribes a reading that renders Japan's interest in learning these ways as part of national efforts to modernize/Westernize quickly. However, this is a narrative that neatly overwrites a more complicated history where the United States advises Japan in its settler colonial nation-building endeavor into the resource-rich lands of the northern island of Hokkaidō—home of the Indigenous Ainu peoples. This history, which seems to be anticipated in Japan's request to "borrow a little" of the United States' light, is one that is still hotly contested in Japan, and Japanese studies, where investments in seeing such undertakings as "domestic" development run deep. Rather than seeing the events that unfolded and the past they call upon as the result of a "natural" and predestined progression or "development," we would be better served by considering them the foreseeable consequences of actions undertaken in the name of nineteenth-century imperial ideologies, modernization, and keeping pace with the West. Maintaining the illusion that settler colonial national successes are not rooted in theft—of Indigenous lands, lives, labor, and resources—requires the active participation of national/international populations in erasing the significance of Indigeneity, the fact of continued Indigenous existence, and the consequences of settler colonialism that continue to be borne by Indigenous communities globally. Insisting on the inconsequence of Indigenous presence and absence (e.g., from citing statistical irrelevance in order to legitimate not collecting or including data about Indigenous peoples, to assertions that there are no more "real" [insert name of existing Indigenous peoples here]) presents itself in a variety of seemingly innocuous ways in settler societies, and any interrogation into how we contribute to the continual vanishing of Native peoples and concerns must begin by addressing this fact.

CONCLUSION

I hope that this article has, at least in some small way, managed to shed light into the shadows where the specters of colonialism work to prevent scholars and lay people alike from seeing or grappling with hidden narratives of the past. For the specters of colonialism work to ensure that historical events are so thoroughly overwritten that the possibility of other narratives emerging has been all but foreclosed—be they by the perceived inevitability and naturalness of Indigenous disappearance, by lamentations that we will never know (justified by claims that documentation does not exist, even when archives can be read in a way that sees beyond the haunted logics of empire to reveal some of the histories that others insist do not exist), or by taking colonial conjecture as embedded in the archives at face value.[17]

Each of the hallmarks of settler colonial success represented in "Our Visitors" is predicated on, and only possible because of, the theft, slaughter, and great violence done to Indigenous peoples. This is a great violence that is perpetuated by our failure to critically account for and engage with Indigeneity, Indigenous presence, and orchestrated Indigenous "absence" in our scholarly work. For when we participate in the vanishing of Indigenous peoples by undermining Native political concerns, by dismissing Native land and resource claims, and by employing tactics to help us to avoid reckoning with what our own complicity in the continued dispossession of Indigenous peoples might mean and bring to the discipline, we are writing on the side of white supremacy.

Ethnic studies scholars and the scholarship we produce are not immune to the influence of the specters of colonialism. Working on ethnic studies subjects and engaging in critical ethnic studies critique alone is not enough to exorcise these haunted logics of empire from where they lay embedded in the colonized landscapes of academic inquiry. However, by working to recognize some of the normalized ways that the specters of colonialism hold sway over our decisions to include Native peoples and experiences, or the way they aid attempts to legitimate our failure to include them, we can begin to remove ourselves, and our scholarship, from their spheres of influence. While there have been efforts to critically think through the disciplinary, theoretical, and political implications of Indigeneity in ethnic studies (as signaled by the "critical" in critical ethnic studies), it has yet to be seen if these efforts would be fleeting or sustained. By working to dispel the power that the specters of colonialism wield, and interrogating the haunted logics of empire, we may succeed in rendering visible the multitude of ways that haunted knowledge about Indigenous peoples is embedded in archives, reinforced in educational systems, and—unless we take action—reproduced in our scholarship.

DANIKA MEDAK-SALTZMAN is assistant professor of ethnic studies at the University of Colorado, Boulder, and author of *Specters of Colonialism: Native Peoples, Visual Cultures, and Colonial Projects in the United States and Japan (1860–1904)* (Minnesota, forthcoming).

NOTES

I would like to thank the press, editorial board, my coeditor, and fellow contributors for their efforts in seeing this issue into print. I am indebted to Penelope M. Kelsey, Shannon A. Mason, and Antonio T. Tiongson Jr. for reading drafts and offering generous and timely comments as I worked on this article.

1. Patrick Wolfe, "Settler Colonialism and the Elimination of the Native," *Journal of Genocide Research* 8, no. 4 (2006): 388.

2. Jodi A. Byrd, *The Transit of Empire: Indigenous Critiques of Colonialism* (Minneapolis: University of Minnesota Press, 2011), 6.

3. I use "appendage" in an analogous way to how Emma Perez frames conventional inclusion of women's histories in *The Decolonial Imaginary: Writing Chicanas into History* (Bloomington: Indiana University Press, 1999), 12.

4. We must treat the failure to incorporate Indigeneity in a sophisticated way as inexcusable, and see doing so as akin to broadcasting one's complicity in furthering settler colonial ideologies that mandate Indigenous disappearance and insist upon the inconsequence of Indigeneity. See Bonita Lawrence and Enakshi Dua, "Decolonizing Antiracism," *Social Justice* 32, no. 4 (2005): 120–43.

5. As Ari Kelman has argued in *A Misplaced Massacre* (Cambridge, Mass.: Harvard University Press, 2013), as Mark Rifkin explored in the second issue (Fall 2014) of *NAIS*, the journal of the Native American and Indigenous Studies Association,

and as Boyd Cothran and Ari Kelman outline in "How the Civil War Became the Indian Wars," *New York Times,* May 25, 2015.

6. See, among others, Tiya Miles, *Ties That Bind* (Berkeley: University of California Press, 2005); and Patricia Penn Hilden, "How the Border Lies," in *Decolonial Voices,* ed. Arturo J. Aldama and Naomi H. Quiñonez (Bloomington: Indiana University Press, 2002).

7. While it is beyond the scope of this article, Jared Sexton's "The *Vel* of Slavery: Tracking the Figure of the Unsovereign" (*Critical Sociology* [December 2014]: 1–15]) provides an excellent example of using a limited understanding of critical Indigenous studies as a whole (in this case through a consideration of one narrow strand of theorizing) to make sweeping claims about the discipline itself—in this case in attempts to levy a charge of complicity with antiblackness. Doing so serves to eclipse (for a Native studies audience, anyway) what valid points he may have and also appears to rank and subordinate histories of suffering. Ultimately this piece seems to reproduce what it intends to critique—namely, that strains of exceptionalism inform both settler colonial critique and antiblackness. For a more comprehensive engagement with this latter sentiment, see Iyko Day's article "Being or Nothingness: Indigeneity, Antiblackness, and Settler Colonial Critique" in this issue.

8. Setsu Shigematsu and Keith L. Camacho, eds., *Militarized Currents: Toward a Decolonized Future in Asia and the Pacific* (Minneapolis: University of Minnesota Press, 2010), xxvi.

9. Avery Gordon, *Ghostly Matters: Haunting and the Sociological Imagination* (Minneapolis: University of Minnesota Press, 1996), 190.

10. Karl Marx and Friedrich Engels, *The Communist Manifesto,* Penguin Little Black Classics 20 (London: Penguin Books, 2015); Jacques Derrida, *Specters of Marx: The State of the Debt, the Work of Mourning, and the New International* (New York: Routledge, 1994).

11. Regarding Japanese intervention into Ainu territory, see, for example: Richard Siddle, *Race, Resistance, and the Ainu of Japan* (New York: Routledge, 1996); Mark J. Hudson, ann-elise lewallen, and Mark K. Watson, eds., *Beyond Ainu Studies: Changing Academic and Public Perspectives* (Honolulu: University of Hawai'i Press, 2014). For discussion of the significance of framing Japan's intervention into Ainu territory as settler colonialism, see Danika Medak-Saltzman, *Specters of Colonialism* (Minneapolis: University of Minnesota Press, forthcoming).

12. Nicole R. Fleetwood, *Troubling Vision: Performance, Visuality, and Blackness* (Chicago: University of Chicago Press, 2011), 16.

13. During its period of seclusion, Japan only allowed restricted trade relationships with the Dutch East India Company in Nagasaki.

14. Benedict Anderson, *Imagined Communities: Reflections on the Origins of Nationalism* (New York: Verso, 1991).

15. Emma LaRoque introduced "civ/sav" as shorthand for the simplistic yet pervasive use of the civilized versus savage dichotomy to explain away colonial violence, justify conquest, and create fact out of prejudiced assumptions about Indigenous intellectual inferiority. Emma LaRoque, "The Metis in English Canadian Literature," *The Canadian Journal of Native Studies* 3, no. 1 (1983): 86.

16. The three papal bulls are *Dum Diversas* of June 18, 1452, and *Romanus Ponti-fex* of January 8, 1455, both issued by Pope Nicholas V, and the *Inter Caetera* issued on May 4, 1493, by Pope Alexander VI.

17. See Michel Rolph Trouillot, *Silencing the Past: Power and the Production of History* (Boston: Beacon Press, 1995); and Danika Medak-Saltzman, "Transnational Indigenous Exchange: Rethinking Global Interactions of Indigenous Peoples at the 1904 St. Louis Exposition," *American Quarterly* 62, no. 3 (September 2010): 591–615.

Afro-Asian Inquiry and the Problematics of Comparative Critique

ANTONIO T. TIONGSON JR.

This article represents a critical engagement with the "comparative turn" in ethnic studies; that is, an interrogation of the broader implications of the ascendancy and valorization of comparative critique as a central category of analysis and an index of contemporary ethnic studies scholarship through a critical consideration of a select body of writing predicated on a comparative approach. Spurred by the perceived inadequacies of a biracial framing and theorizing of race and racialization (i.e., the so-called black/white paradigm), thinking comparatively has become an imperative to the project of ethnic studies, heralding a paradigmatic and analytic shift and inaugurating what one cultural analyst describes as a new stage in the evolution of ethnic studies, "one long postponed by a standoff between a multiracial model limited by a national horizon and a diasporic model that lacked historical ground for conducting cross-racial analysis."[1]

As a number of race and ethnic studies scholars posit, comparative analysis is increasingly viewed as indispensable to the project of ethnic studies. In an edited volume titled *Black and Brown in Los Angeles: Beyond Conflict and Coalition,* for example, Josh Kun and Laura Pulido make the point that comparative ethnic studies has emerged "as a substantive field within the discipline of ethnic studies itself," generating a fairly robust and rapidly expanding archive of comparative scholarship.[2] Echoing these remarks, Marta E. Sanchez speaks of "the renaissance of comparative studies of race and ethnicity" that foregrounds the intertwined and interconnected histories of racialized groups.[3] The purchase accorded this kind of work is reflected in the spate of publications that can be described as fundamentally comparative in their scope.[4] It is reflected in the way this approach has become incorporated into mission statements of prominent ethnic studies programs across the nation.[5] "Conventional" approaches, in other words, have given way to comparative approaches that, on the surface, seem to provide a more textured analysis of the dynamics of race and the intricacies of the racialization process.

In this article, I delineate and call into question the core assumptions and claims made in the name of comparative critique within the context of ethnic studies and ethnic studies scholarship. I focus specifically on Afro-Asian literature, a burgeoning body of writing that is instructive in terms of speaking to and shedding light on the promises and perils of comparative critique. While it is not the only body of writing engaged in comparative critique, it is arguably the most prominent strand of this literature, accruing a great deal of purchase and prestige as evidenced by the profound growth of this field of inquiry. Accordingly, Afro-Asian inquiry provides an ideal starting point from which to interrogate what is to be gained by engaging in comparative critique but also what are the limitations of performing this kind of critique. I argue that notwithstanding the currency of Afro-Asian literature, this body of writing has yet to grapple substantively with the complications and challenges attendant to comparative critique. In short, Afro-Asian inquiry has given rise to a set of issues and concerns pertaining to the contours and trajectory of comparative critique that has yet to be adequately addressed and rigorously explored, issues and concerns that drive this article.

To illustrate, relatively scant or no attention has been paid to currents and concerns that serve to trouble the underlying assumptions and core claims of much of this body of writing. For example, Afro-Asian inquiry has largely been framed in terms of what Helen H. Jun has described in another context as "a teleological investment in 'interracial solidarity'"[6]—the sort of investment that delimits the terrain from which to engage in comparative critique. Moreover, much of the literature is predicated on the need to transcend the black-white binary, a premise problematized by a cohort of critical race and ethnic studies scholars who take Afro-Asian inquiry to task for misconstruing the broader significance and relevance of the paradigm. Another critique I take up in this article is the manner in which Afro-Asian inquiry invokes Indigeneity in ways that ultimately serve to obscure the specificities of the status of Native peoples and perpetuate the sanctioned ignorance surrounding Native issues and concerns.

Rather than take for granted the value of thinking comparatively, then, this article strives to spotlight and problematize the theoretical and political investments of Afro-Asian studies. Turning to Afro-Asian inquiry as an occasion to think about what constitutes comparative critique, I will argue that the comparative turn in ethnic studies has *not* necessarily given way to a more nuanced understanding of the dynamics of race and the intricacies of the racialization process. Instead, it has given rise to a distinct set of provocations that has yet to be adequately addressed. To put the matter somewhat differently, I question the proposition that a comparative frame or lens represents an unquestioned and unqualified advance over previous approaches in the field. Ultimately, my concern in this article is to articulate points of departure for more rigorously and profoundly engaging in comparative critique through a critical consideration of emergent intellectual currents that pose challenges and complications to Afro-Asian inquiry. I will proceed, first, by delineating what constitutes comparative critique and then establishing the scope of Afro-Asian inquiry via a consideration of recurrent strands of inquiry that comprise this body of writing. I then spell out the problematics of comparative critique through a consideration of currents and concerns emanating from various fields of study and raised by a number of scholars, currents and concerns that unsettle the underlying assumptions and core claims of this body of writing.

SPECIFYING THE SCOPE OF COMPARATIVE SCHOLARSHIP

As a number of critical race and ethnic studies scholars point out, the comparative turn in the study of race and ethnicity marks a departure for ethnic studies in terms of its scope of inquiry, centering on relations among minoritized groups rather than on relations between whites and minoritized groups. In the words of Laura Pulido: "Although comparative research within ethnic studies is hardly new, scholars have only recently begun seriously theorizing differences and relationships between various racial/ethnic groups."[7] Pulido goes on to make the point that there is a growing realization among contemporary critical race and ethnic studies scholars "that individual groups could not be understood in isolation,"[8] paving the way for scholarship that attempts to capture what Andrew F. Jones and Nikhil Pal Singh describe as "the wide-ranging social and political relations between margin and margin."[9] Traise Yamamoto endorses such a move because of the way it provides a corrective to what she describes as a dearth of vocabulary that does justice to the intricacies of relations among groups of color: "And the trauma of American race relations, as with all trauma, is that there is really no language for talking about what happens between communities of color, for talking about how racialization happens between people of color."[10] Covering similar ground, John D. Márquez speaks of a critical ethnic studies paradigm that foregrounds how racial injustice exceeds the bounds of a particular minoritized group experience.[11] For these scholars, a comparative analytic is seen as crucial to sorting out complex racial dynamics not just between whites and minoritized groups of color but also among minoritized groups of color, and how these groups are positioned relative to each other in a mutually constitutive manner.

In terms of the impetus for comparative critique, Susan Koshy looks to the current moment as necessitating a shift in the lens we deploy in our analysis of race. In her view, the comparative turn is a necessary development because of the imperatives of what she describes as the "new conjuncture" that is no longer predicated "on a structural divide between racial minorities and whites." Instead, it is now marked by an "axis of stratification [that] has multiplied and shifted so that it runs within and between marginalized and dominant identities, reconfiguring them in unprecedented ways."[12] Accordingly, we have seen calls to engage in comparative work as a way to disrupt what Koshy describes as "the axiomatic status of whiteness as the referent against which minority subjects define themselves and others," paving the way for scholarship that decenters whiteness as the analytical referent for the study of race and ethnicity. For Koshy, the implications of this shift demand a move toward an analytic of interracialism that, in turn, "necessitates a comparative turn, a move from specifying the boundaries and internal heterogeneity of particular groups to an understanding of their interarticulation."[13] Recalling Stuart Hall's notion of conjuncture, Koshy makes a case for coming up with paradigms that can account for the particularities of the current era marked by the reshaping of the racial landscape and the ascendancy of neoliberalism.[14]

What, exactly, constitutes comparative scholarship remains an open question yet attempts to define the bounds of this kind of work revolved around a particular set of theoretical concerns and investments. At its core, comparative critique aims to broaden the ground from which to consider the dynamics of the racialization process, accentuating the ways in which racialization operates in a *relational* manner. An underlying premise of contemporary ethnic studies scholarship is that a critical engagement with race necessitates comparative thinking and that racialization is an inherently comparative process and a relational term. Scholars engaged in this kind of work, however, make a concerted effort to veer away from simply delineating "similarities and differences" among racialized groups and instead emphasize the interconstitutive nature of the racialization process that, in turn, necessitates comparative critique. In the following, Grace Kyungwon Hong provides a definition of comparative racialization, which encapsulates this aspect of the racialization process.

"Comparative racialization" in its most basic definition refers to scholarship that addresses African American, Asian American, Native/indigenous and Chicana/o racializations as occurring in relation to each other. Yet this work does not merely articulate commonalities between communities of color but poses a more complex question about how a focus on differences between and within racialized groups might enable us to imagine alternative modes of coalition.[15]

For Hong, viable comparative approaches "do not merely take 'African American,' 'Asian American,' 'Chicano,' and so on as knowable and internally coherent, nationally based categories that can be compared." Instead, Hong considers these racial formations as "internally contradictory and uneven."[16]

Similarly, for Shu-mei Shih, the meaning of comparison does not simply reside in "the arbitrary juxtaposition of two terms in difference and similarity" but rather in the foregrounding and bringing forth of "submerged or displaced relationalities into view" to reveal "these relationalities as the starting point for a fuller understanding of racialization as a comparative process."[17] In making a distinction between the different modes of comparison, Shih stresses the importance of grappling with "the conjuncture of time and place" in any sort of viable comparative project.[18] In her view,

> Because instances of racialization are situated in specific times and places, comparison between these instances may seem random or unrelated, but the colonial turn reveals potential and concrete relations among them. To think comparatively therefore is to think about the world where the colonial turn has left indelible marks—that is, to think the worldliness of race.[19]

Here Shih situates her analysis of the racialization process within the context of colonialism, drawing on Frantz Fanon's work to tease out her thinking on what a project of comparison entails. Shih is particularly interested in how Fanon conceptualized comparison as an inherent feature of colonial society that is fundamental to the dynamics of racialization in both the colony and the metropole.[20]

In *How Race Is Made in America: Immigration, Citizenship, and the Historical Power of Racial Scripts*, Natalia Molina makes a case for relational analysis because of the way such an approach attends to the ways race operates in a mutually constitutive manner. In Molina's words:

By *relational,* I do not mean *comparative.* A comparative treatment of race compares and contrasts groups, treating them as independent of one another; a relational treatment recognizes that race is a mutually constitutive process and thus attends to how, when, where, and to what extent groups intersect. It recognizes that there are limits to examining racialized groups in isolation.[21]

Drawing on and extending Michael Omi and Howard Winant's work on racial formation, Molina advances the idea of studying the interconnections among different racialized groups and racial projects.[22] In the case of the racialization of Mexicans, this process unfolded in a matrix that also ensnared the racialization of other groups across time and space.

Similar to Molina, David Theo Goldberg makes a distinction between different modes of comparative analysis, what he describes as a comparativist account and a relational account. Goldberg is particularly interested in the capacity of each mode of analysis to shed light on the workings of race and racism.

A comparativist account undertakes to reveal through analogy; a relational account reveals through indicating how effects are brought about as a result of historical, political or economic, legal or cultural links, the one acting upon another. A comparativist account may choose to contrast racially conceived or ordered relations of production in one place and another. A relational analysis will stress the (re-)production of relational ties and their mutually effecting and reinforcing impacts. A comparativist account contrasts and compares. A relational account connects.[23]

For Goldberg, a comparativist frame is problematic given how this mode of analysis has been bracketed and delimited by a focus on national contexts and dynamics and, therefore, cannot account for the full complexity of race and racism. Echoing Shih's assertion about the importance of grappling with "the conjuncture of time and place," Goldberg asserts that claims emanating from comparativist accounts are necessarily limited because these claims cannot account for how race and racisms are mutually constituted across time and space.

In contradistinction, Goldberg finds a relational approach more illuminating and revealing because of the way it provides a fuller and more comprehensive account of the workings of race and racism. In Goldberg's view, "a relational account accordingly reveals something not otherwise comprehensible." He goes on to make the point that such an approach "signals how state formations or histories, logics of oppression and exploitation are linked, whether causally or symbolically, ideationally or semantically."[24] Unlike comparative approaches, then, relational approaches do not operate from the presumption of boundaries or what Goldberg describes as the "supposed discreteness of the compared elements" but rather from the connectedness of seemingly discrete cases.[25] For Goldberg, relational accounts are particularly useful because they offer an optics that throws into sharp relief the ways racial dynamics in one place are constitutive of racial dynamics in other places.[26]

The editors of the anthology *Strange Affinities: The Gender and Sexual Politics of Comparative Racialization* also make a distinction between different modes of comparative analysis in endeavoring to proffer an alternative genealogy of ethnic studies rooted in a women of color feminism and queer of color critique. Alluding to the comparative and internationalist origins of ethnic studies, Grace Kyungwon Hong and Roderick A. Ferguson identify the stakes for thinking through an alternative comparative analytic suited to the contemporary moment, noting that

> the stakes for identifying new comparative models are immensely high, for the changing configurations of power in the era after the decolonizing movements and new social movements of the mid-twentieth century demand that we understand how particular populations are rendered vulnerable to processes of death and devaluation over and against other populations, in ways that palimpsestically register older modalities of racialized death but also exceed them.[27]

For Hong and Ferguson, there is much at stake in generating alternative analytics that do not reproduce the problematic tendencies and logic of various modes of comparison including dominant and nationalist modes of comparison. For example, they take issue with minority nationalisms for recapitulating the logic of discreteness undergirding the dominant mode of comparison. In their critique of normative models, Hong and Ferguson look to women of color feminism and queer of color critique as providing an alternative model for realizing the potential of a critical comparative race scholarship that is attentive and attuned to the material conditions of racial and colonial violence. They look to these critical formations "as comparative analytics rather than descriptions of identity categories" that serve to illuminate contemporary processes of valuations and the interrelatedness of race, gender, and sexuality.[28] Ultimately, Hong and Ferguson also endorse a relational comparative analytic that centers difference, contradictions, and heterogeneities and forges a language that captures "what cannot be known, what escapes articulation."[29] For these aforementioned authors, relationality constitutes an advance over comparativity in the way it sheds light on processes of valuation in the current conjuncture, processes that exceed the bounds and logic of nation.

THE EMERGENT FIELD OF AFRO-ASIAN INQUIRY

The field of Afro-Asian studies constitutes a rapidly growing field as evidenced by the proliferation of works on Afro-Asian interconnections as well as a number of special issues of journals such as *positions* and *Journal of Asian American Studies* centering on different facets of Afro-Asian relations.[30] For scholars pursuing this kind of work, the aim is to uncover hitherto buried or obscured historical convergences between people of African and Asian descent on a global scale in order to do justice to the intricacies of this relationship. For example, the editors of the anthology *Afro Asia: Revolutionary Political and Cultural Connections between African Americans and Asian Americans* strive to render intelligible "the full range of important historical, political, and cultural connections between Asian Americans and African Americans," connections that are not assimilable into conventional narratives of African diasporic history or Asian diasporic history.[31]

Scholars engaged in this kind of work look to the history of encounters between the two groups as a largely underexplored and undertheorized archive that serves as an important vehicle for imagining and cultivating an anti-imperialist political outlook and vision. Afro-Asian scholars, in other words, are engaged in an intellectual and political project of recuperation centered on the recovery of an archive of solidarity between the two groups. Carolyn Rody describes the archive this way:

> This archive is the history of social, cultural, and literary relations between Asian and African Americans, framed by "AfroAsianist" scholars as two peoples who share not only the fact of (differing) racialized, minoritized, American experiences and the mutual possession of long, rich, and sophisticated cultural and expressive traditions, but also a history of productive interaction.[32]

In essence, Afro-Asian encounters constitute an archive that speaks to a "tradition of cross-cultural unity" that has largely been expunged from standard historical accounts.[33] For Fred Ho and Bill V. Mullen, "Afro-Asia" serves as "a strategic intersection for thinking through an internationalist, global paradigm that joins the world's two largest continents and populations, as well as an anti-imperialist, insurgent identity that is no longer majority white in orientation." For these scholars, Afro Asia constitutes "the imperative to imagine a 'new world' grounded upon two great ancient worlds as well as a radical and revolutionary anti-imperialist tradition."[34]

Afro-Asian literature looks specifically to culture and politics as important sites of shared practices and traditions between the two groups. As Ho and Mullen put it, "African Americans and Asian Americans have mutually influenced, borrowed from, and jointly innovated new forms in culture (from music to cuisine to clothing) and politics (from shared movement ideologies to organizations)."[35] In uncovering this archive, scholars aim to trouble the way relations between the two groups have been historically configured as inherently antagonistic. The editors of *AfroAsian Encounters*, for example, make the point that "across the Americas, these two groups have often been thought of as occupying radically incommensurable cultural and political positions."[36] Afro-Asian studies scholars are particularly leery of the preoccupation with the so-called black-Asian conflict because of the way it deflects attention away from the culpability of white supremacy. Accordingly, Afro-Asian literature is motivated by the need to recast and reconfigure this relationship and, in the process, bring to light an alternative genealogy of Afro-Asian relations and the necessity of engaging in comparative critique: "At the least, the coalitional imperative of today's variant of Afro-Asianism is making ever more explicit the degree to which the Asian as a racial concept requires comparative thinking. The Asian American, which is surely the premier example of a racial concept of the Asian, has always been a comparative identity."[37]

The primary catalyst for this kind of work is disenchantment with existing racial paradigms—specifically the black/white paradigm—predicated on biracial theorizing and logic. Edward J. W. Park and John S. W. Park, for example, make the point that existing racial paradigms cannot begin to account for shifting demographics in the United States.

Yet, while American society confronts multiracial realities, much of recent American race theory either dismisses the significance of these groups altogether, or subsumes them into traditional biracial models. The newcomers are neither "Black" nor "White," but they are still characterized in those terms, and this tendency impedes the development of new and compelling ways to examine current race relations. We live in a multiracial society, but we seem stuck in biracial thinking.[38]

For Park and Park, then, race theory in the guise of the black/white paradigm has not kept up with complex racial dynamics and realities and, in particular, the centrality of Asian Americans and Latin@s in terms of shaping the racial landscape of the United States. Instead, extant race theory obscures the specificities of these groups, rendering the experiences of Asian Americans interchangeable with that of whites and Latin@s with that of blacks. In the view of Park and Park, race theorists need to bridge the "gap between how race is theorized and how race is lived" and come up with a more exhaustive theory of race and ethnicity not wedded to a biracial framing.[39]

This has become a fairly standard critique among a cohort of race and ethnic studies scholars especially concerned with the way the paradigm fails to account for the complexities of the contemporary racial landscape as well as the intricacies of interethnic and interracial relations. LeiLani Nishime explains:

> Race in America has largely been understood as a matter of black and white. Even academic conceptual frames tend to emphasize the dichotomies between the colonizer and the colonized, the center and the periphery. Yet it is becoming increasingly obvious that these binaries cannot encompass the experience of many Americans, particularly Asian Americans, who have always occupied the spaces between white and black America.[40]

Shirley Hune speaks of the black/white paradigm as "the predominant racial model" that has been rendered obsolete by shifting racial dynamics. In the following, Hune makes the case for a reconfiguration of the dominant race relations paradigm in a way that can address the realities and needs of non-white, nonblack groups from a public policy perspective. In her view, a paradigm shift entails attending "to the reality of the nation's racial complexity." Such a paradigm shift "will *include* Asian Pacific Americans, Latinos/Latinas, American Indians and other groups in American public policy."[41] She goes on to make the point that the black/white paradigm detracts focus away from "minority-minority" relations that has served to undermine efforts to build alliances among communities of color. Instead, Hune calls for what she describes as a "multiplicity paradigm" that is more suited to account for racial dynamics within a multiracial context.[42]

Michael Omi makes a similar point about the limitations of the black/white paradigm; namely, its failure to account for the nuances of racial tensions: "And what is increasingly evident is that such racial tensions are no longer intelligible, if indeed they ever were, within the framework of a 'black/white' paradigm of race relations." He goes on to assert, "Such biracial theorizing misses the complex nature of race relations in the post-civil rights era and is unable to grasp the patterns of conflict and accommodation among several increasingly large racial/ethnic groups."[43] For scholars engaged in Afro-Asian scholarship, then, an imperative is to generate language that exceeds the bounds of the black/white paradigm because of the way it obscures the specificities of Asian American racial formations. In this line of analysis, therefore, a nuanced accounting of contemporary racial dynamics is predicated on the transcendence of the black/white paradigm.

Gary Y. Okihiro's work is significant in this regard because it would prove to be generative to the emergence of Afro-Asian literature, initially framing and continuing to frame the field's scope of inquiry. His work provides an engagement with the black/white paradigm "that locates Asians (and American Indians and Latinos) somewhere along the divide between black and white. Asians, thus, are 'nearly whites' or 'just like blacks.'"[44] Okihiro is particularly interested in uncovering and foregrounding the shared experiences between Asians and blacks and the broader implications of uncovering historical convergences between the two groups: "We are a kindred people, forged in the fire of white supremacy and struggle, but how can we recall that kinship when our memories have been massaged by white hands, and how can we remember the past when our storytellers have been whispering amid the din of Western civilization and Anglo-conformity?"[45] For Okihiro, then, it is imperative to render what he describes as "kinship" intelligible, a kinship that has been compromised by the machinations of white supremacy. In his work, Okihiro accentuates moments of cooperation between the two groups and the need to render these moments in a readily comprehensible way, what he describes as "acts of antiracialism and solidarity between Asian and African Americans."[46] At the same time, Okihiro attempts to grapple with the complexities of Afro-Asian interconnections.

By seeing only black and white, the presence and absence of all color, whites render Asians, American Indians, and Latinos invisible, ignoring the gradations and complexities of the full spectrum between racial poles. At the same time, Asians share with Africans the status and repression of non-whites—as the Other—and therein lies the debilitating aspect of Asian–African antipathy and the liberating nature of African–Asian unity.[47]

What Okihiro speaks to here is the intricacies of black–Asian American relations rooted in their shared marginalized status without glossing over the differences and distinctions between the two groups. Nonetheless, in much of his work, the point of emphasis is on the links between the two groups and the broader historiographic and political implications of coming to terms with the shared status between the two groups.[48]

THE VARIOUS STRANDS OF AFRO-ASIAN LITERATURE

Within Afro-Asian literature, two moments in particular—the Bandung Conference in 1955 and the Los Angeles riots in 1992—constitute foundational and consequential moments in terms of delimiting the field's scope of inquiry in an overdetermined manner. The Los Angeles riots constitute a particularly vexed moment that has generated a body of work aimed at providing a corrective to extant popular and media accounts of the uprising that conceive of Afro-Asian relations in terms of conflicts and tensions and specifically position African Americans and Asian Americans as inherently antagonistic. As Amy Abugo Ongiri phrases it:

> Images of the "Black-Korean conflict," debates around affirmative action, and "model minority" mythmaking create African Americans and Asian Americans as polar opposites ever doomed to conflict in America's racial ideological landscape. These cultural imaginings disavow even the possibility of cultural exchange occurring at or within the margins of dominant society.[49]

Scholars are especially critical of the deployment of the rubric of "racial conflict" or more specifically "black-Korean conflict" as the dominant interpretive framework to construe Afro-Asian relations because of the way it pits one group against the other and precludes consideration of exchanges and encounters that exceed the bounds of this rubric. For Afro-Asian scholars, the Los Angeles riots acutely reveal the inadequacy of the black/white paradigm because the multicultural nature of the riots cannot be reduced to simple black-Korean encounters.

As a corrective to such popular and media accounts of the Los Angeles riots, a strand of literature has emerged that aims to resignify "Afro-Asian," rendering it alternatively as a term that denotes an "anticolonial, antiracist, and anti-imperialist" stance.[50] In this strand of Afro-Asian literature, the Bandung Conference occupies a prominent place, conventionally configured as the apogee of expressions and instances of solidarity between blacks and Asians. In the words of Nami Kim: "To many, the Bandung era of Afro-Asian solidarity represented a high point of the anti-imperialist and anti-racist struggles of people of Asian and African descent."[51] For Vijay Prashad, Bandung serves as a "major inspiration as well as an epistemological framework" to cultivate an anti-colonialist politics global in scope.[52] The prominence of Bandung speaks to how "'AfroAsian' studies have always been energized by a coalitional spirit, a reparative, antiracist urge."[53] In the following, Ho and Mullen underscore the import and indispensability of Bandung in any efforts to engage in Afro-Asian inquiry: "Bandung informs and haunts any and all efforts to theorize Afro Asia. It is both the watershed and highwater mark of black-Asian affiliation and the unfinished and imperfect dream of a road still being pursued and paved by the authors represented in this book."[54] For these scholars, Bandung looms large in terms of serving as a potentially generative site that speaks to the (unfulfilled) promise and potential of Afro-Asian solidarity, casting Afro-Asian relations in the language of racial solidarity.[55]

Another strand of this literature aims to render intelligible the ways the racialization history of African Americans bears on the racialization history of Asian Americans. The underlying assumption is that "Asian American" and "African American" are mutually constitutive categories of analysis and that the racialization of Asian Americans is mediated and refracted by the racialization of African Americans. Najia Aarim-Heriot's work is instructive in this regard, namely her focus on how the "Negro" problem is inextricably linked to the Chinese question. She grounds her analysis of the Chinese exclusion movement in nineteenth-century America race relations, specifically black/white relations, arguing that anti-Chinese sentiment was rooted in antiblack sentiment. In other words, antiblackness served as a precursor and precedent for antipathy directed at the Chinese during this period.[56]

In *Interracial Encounters: Reciprocal Representations in African and Asian American Literatures, 1896–1937,* Julia H. Lee strives to intervene in the dominant framing of Afro-Asian relations "as irrevocably antagonistic or romanticized as intrinsically linked by a shared history of racism" through a consideration of representations of Afro-Asian relations in a variety of African American and Asian American texts.[57] For Lee, either claim is problematic because of the way it operates according to the same essentializing logic and speaks to the necessity of a comparative approach because "it can deepen and enrich our notions of what makes up American literature as well as present us with an array of compelling and significant alternative literary histories that do not fit easily or at all into the norms or the canonical narrative."[58]

In the case of Helen Heran Jun, she is concerned with how the construction of Asian Americans was contingent on the construction of African Americans "in relation to the shifting terrains of citizenship, the labor market, and U.S. national culture."[59] Utilizing what she describes as a relational framework, her objective is to unveil how "Asian Americans and African Americans have been unevenly defined in relation to each other and that in their respective struggles for inclusion, they both have had to negotiate the terms by which the other has been racially excluded."[60] Jun examines the contradictions that mark the institution of citizenship and how these contradictions are negotiated in a wide array of African American and Asian American cultural texts as well as the ways Asian American and African American claims to citizenship are mutually constitutive.[61]

Attention has also been directed at cultural exchanges between African Americans and Asian Americans particularly in the realm of music, film, and theater. According to this body of work, culture serves as one of the most compelling sites for the examination of black-Asian dynamics. A point of emphasis is not just the influence of African American culture on Asian American cultural practices but also the influence of Asian culture on black cultural practices.[62] Deborah Elizabeth Whaley, for instance, examines how African Americans are engaged in some form of Orientalism within the context of hip hop. In her words, "Given the subjugation of Black Americans within hegemonic power relations and the assumption of our identity as always-already stable and fixed, what does it mean when Black hip-hop musicians seek to obscure their Black skin with yellow masks?"[63] Whaley examines how this dynamic plays out in the realm of visual culture and the implications of this kind of performance for forging Afro-Asian solidarity.

For Deborah Wong, performance constitutes a compelling site for the interrogation of the permutations of African American/Asian American relations. She suggests that the performative is a particularly vexed site, opening up possibilities for cross-identification between the two groups but also serving to bolster power relations. According to Wong, "While these performative meeting grounds between Asian American and African American performers are potential sites for new social realities and new political sensibilities, other intersections suggest daring and problematic experiments with ventriloquism."[64] Also published in the same special issue of the *Journal of Asian American Studies,* Amy Abugo Ongiri raises the question of what it means for African Americans to draw on signifiers of Asian and Asian American culture. She is particularly interested in African American reception of and identification with the kung fu film genre as a potentially productive site for the examination of the intricacies that mark relations between the two groups but also "instances of slippage and indeterminacy in which notions of the totalitarian nature of power and western notions of aesthetics, culture, and dominance are undone."[65]

AFRO-ASIAN LITERATURE AND THE POSSIBILITIES OF COMPARATIVE CRITIQUE

Afro-Asian inquiry seems to embody the potential and promise of comparative critique, performing a number of critical interventions. Specifically, this body of literature has mounted what appear to be powerful critiques against approaches wedded to a biracial framing, seemingly offering a more nuanced frame for making sense of complex racial dynamics that exceed the bounds of this kind of framing. Additionally, Afro-Asian inquiry's centering of relations between groups of color serves to undermine the normative status of whiteness as the analytical referent for the study of race. At the same time, it brings to the fore a largely ignored or overlooked history of Afro-Asian encounters and exchanges that serves as a powerful counter to white supremacy predicated on pitting minoritized groups against one another. In doing so, Afro-Asian inquiry has wielded new ways of imagining relations between groups previously viewed as having mutually exclusive histories, making a compelling case that Afro-Asian relations cannot be construed in terms of a zero sum game or under the rubric of "racial conflict."

Nami Kim directs our attention to another potential payoff of Afro-Asian inquiry, making the case that a consideration of Afro-Asian relations may very well pave the way for serious consideration of other relational dynamics such as "Asian-Latino/a, Asian-Native, Afro-Asian-Latino/a, and Afro-Asian-Native connections" that can generate "similar critiques of racism, imperialism, and American nationalism."[66] Moreover, this body of writing seems ideally suited to place disciplinary formations with distinct histories, imperatives, and concerns in critical dialogue with one another, thus challenging the parochialisms and conventions of fields like African American studies and Asian American studies. In short, Afro-Asian literature constitutes a significant intervention in the way it gestures toward further areas of inquiry that are potentially transformative theoretically, politically, and disciplinarily. But while it is certainly important to pay attention to the lines of inquiry opened up by this body of writing, it is also important to not lose sight of the set of issues raised by this body of writing, issues that have yet to be addressed in a sustained and critical manner.

ON THE PROBLEMATICS OF COMPARATIVE CRITIQUE

One such issue raised by Afro-Asian literature revolves around the investment in documenting and establishing moments of Afro-Asian cross-identification that could then serve as a basis of multiracial solidarity between the two groups. Most of these efforts are predicated on what Lye describes as "Asian American analogical dependency," a notion of Afro-Asian analogy that hinges on the assumption that Asian Americans and African Americans occupy analogous historical and political positions.[67] Cultural critics like Traise Yamamoto, however, caution that "within this framework, cross-identification of Asian Americans can work not to undermine existing racial structures but rather to reinforce them."[68] In the foregoing, Yamamoto alludes to the way cross-racial identification in and of itself cannot guarantee the undercutting of racial hierarchies. Instead, what constitutes the nature of cross-racial identification—its terms and basis—must be specified.

The field's investment in a narrative of cross-racial solidarity is very much evident in the way it valorizes the Bandung Conference as an originary moment in Afro-Asian solidarity in terms of establishing the grounds for cultivating a vision of anticolonial politics. This sort of investment, however, is contingent on a rather narrow and idealized reading of the significance of Bandung that informs popular understandings of the 1955 conference. As Antoinette Burton describes it: "If North Americans know about Bandung at all, they most often apprehend it through the lens of histories of racial solidarity and cross-racial possibility of the kind that Richard Wright captured in his eyewitness account of the conference."[69] As Burton alludes to, however, this reading of Bandung serves to uphold what she describes as "the romance of racialism that haunts many accounts of Banding and its aftermath," a romance that I argue haunts Afro-Asian inquiry in the way Bandung is embedded in a triumphalist and teleological narrative even as a number of Afro-Asian scholars voice their concerns about the dangers of idealizing

Afro-Asian relations.[70] Along similar lines, Colleen Lye raises the question of "whether the retrieval of Third Worldist genealogies accomplishes something more than a nostalgic response to the rise of Asian capitalism on a world scale and to the thinning claim of Asian American intellectuals to any representative function."[71]

As Helen Heran Jun posits, there are analytical constraints to scholarship organized around a frame and discourse of cross-racial solidarity. In making the point that a significant strand of comparative ethnic studies projects are wedded to an analysis predicated on a narrow frame (i.e., an axis of identification-disidentification, resistance-complicity, or hegemonic-counterhegemonic), Jun directs our attention to what is obscured in this kind of analysis; namely, the complex entanglements of Asian American and African American racial formations that exceed the bounds of cross-racial solidarity. Rather than emphasize the resistant or the oppositional, Jun instead endeavors to provide an alternative comparative analytic, one that can better account for "how historically specific contradictions inherent in the institution of citizenship take shape and are negotiated in Asian American and African American cultural production."[72] She goes against the grain of the trajectory of much of Afro-Asian scholarship that is predicated on the recovery of instances of interracial solidarity between African Americans and Asians and employs an interpretive strategy that evaluates a text for its reproduction ("complicity") or rupture ("resistance") of existing social relations. In so doing, Jun broadens the scope of inquiry of African American and Asian American racial formations.[73]

Another issue revolves around what has become a matter of course in Afro-Asian inquiry, the presumption of the need to transcend the black/white paradigm given its purported obsolescence. According to Lye:

> Racial, racialized, but lacking the certainty of a racial formation, the Asian American's attenuated relation to racial conceptualization can be seen in the extent to which critical focus on the Asian American is so often couched in terms of "needing to move beyond race as a matter of black and white." The Asian American is more easily evoked as a third term to trouble binary habits of racial classification and analysis than to illustrate the genuine multiplicity of racial logics and racisms.[74]

Accordingly, much of the literature is driven by the need to displace the black/white paradigm because of its apparent lack of sophistication and inability to provide a nuanced account of contemporary racial dynamics precipitated by shifting racial dynamics in which African Americans are no longer the majority group of color. Critics also take issue with the way the black/white paradigm serves to undermine efforts at coalition-building in its privileging of antiblackness as the basis for coalition. For these critics, the black/white paradigm is especially detrimental to Asian Americans and Latin@s because of the way it obscures their distinct experiences with racism. In other words, antiblack racism serves as *the* paradigmatic form of racism, distorting how other communities of color experience racism as well as expressions of racism between communities of color. Any sort of invocation of the black/white paradigm, therefore, is seen as necessarily suspect and problematic.[75]

A cohort of critical race and ethnic studies scholars, however, take issue with exhortations to go beyond black and white because of the way these calls summarily misconstrue the broader significance and relevance of the black/white paradigm. Jared Sexton, for instance, views critiques of the black/white paradigm as based on a profound misconceptualization of the paradigm itself.

> However, the notion of an "endemic" black-white model of racial thought is something of a social fiction—one might say a *misreading*—that depends upon a reduction of the sophistication of the paradigm in question. Once that reduction is performed, the fiction can be deployed for a range of political and intellectual purposes.[76]

For Katerina Deliovsky and Tamari Kitossa, calls to abandon the black/white paradigm are predicated on a failure to grapple with the way antiblackness "gives shape and context to the oppression of other racially marginalized groups, while creating a qualitatively distinct oppression for African-descended peoples."[77] Along similar lines, Janine Young Kim notes how the paradigm serves as a context for the marginalization of nonblack people of color, asserting that "the black/white paradigm is not one that we can escape through our own will."[78] John D. Márquez also subscribes to a broad understanding of blackness, what he terms foundational blackness, as a way to accentuate how blackness has profoundly shaped and continues to shape Latin@ politics and subjectivities. In his view, then, blackness (and for that matter antiblackness) has relevance beyond black bodies in terms of anchoring Latin@ subject and oppositional formations.[79]

For this cohort of scholars, efforts to displace the black/white paradigm are problematic because they are predicated on a particular reading of the black/white paradigm that serves to blur the foundational status of blackness. Put another way, these efforts are marred by reductive notions of blackness, obscuring the specificity of blackness in terms of its enduring significance that extends beyond black people or black bodies and shifting demographics.[80] Moreover, these scholars take issue with how conventional critiques of the black/white paradigm pathologize and position blackness as an anathema to effective multiracial solidarity building, something to be overcome because of its political obsolescence. These critics raise critically important questions that Afro-Asian inquiry has yet to engage with in a sustained and substantive manner, a lack of engagement that includes a questioning of what it means to dispense with the black/white paradigm, what the repercussions of such a move might be and what, exactly, constitutes an alternative paradigm, and how this paradigm might represent an advance over the black/white paradigm. For these scholars, the challenge is not dispensing with but grappling with the broader significance and relevance of the paradigm and the pervasiveness of antiblackness.

A third issue has to do with the way Afro-Asian inquiry invokes Indigeneity to accentuate the purported limits of the black-white binary and bolster its critique of the paradigm. Specifically, in what have become conventional exhortations against the black/white paradigm within the field, Native peoples are invoked as yet another group overlooked by the paradigm along with Asian Pacific Americans and Latin@s with the effect of collapsing Indigenous peoples with these other groups. Native peoples, in other words, are positioned as yet another "minority" group subsumed under the category of "people of color," predicated on what Enakshi Dua has described in another context as a politics of commonality that serves to flatten substantive and incommensurable differences among colonized and racialized groups.[81] In the case of Park and Park, their lack of acknowledgment of Native peoples evacuates Indigenous subjects of contemporaneity and occludes their ongoing struggles for self-determination.[82]

As Indigenous studies scholars have endeavored to point out, however, Native peoples are more appropriately construed as a colonized group who are also members of sovereign nations. These scholars assert that the categorization of Native peoples as "ethnic minorities" is tantamount to a form of colonialism because of the way it obscures fundamental differences between Native peoples and people of color including their distinct relationship to the land. Winona Stevenson writes, "Given the current political climate surrounding Aboriginal self-government and land rights, the continued act of 'naming' us 'ethnic' can only be understood as colonialist."[83]

For Stevenson, a viable comparative project needs to situate Native peoples in relation to other Native peoples around the globe rather than with non-Native people of color in order to avoid collapsing the overlapping yet distinct processes of racialization and colonization.

This lack of critical engagement is symptomatic of the neglect of settler colonialism as an analytic frame within Afro-Asian inquiry and, more generally, Asian American studies. It speaks to the field's inability to grapple with the settler state and the embrace of raced frameworks that ultimately serves to minoritize Native peoples, raced frameworks that "depend upon an historical aphasia of the conquest of indigenous peoples."[84] More broadly, it speaks to the field's lack of critical engagement with Native American and Indigenous studies, including what are considered core claims in the project of critical Native American and Indigenous studies. In other words, in this body of writing, there is no space for a serious and substantive engagement with Indigenous critiques of the logics of genocide and colonialism and the complicity of Afro-Asian inquiry with settler colonialist logics and assumptions.

Shu-mei Shih frames this myopia as a function of how calls to go beyond the black-white binary have resulted in new insights on particular groups but not on others. More specifically, she posits that the emergent scholarship on comparative racialization has not brought the case of Native peoples into sustained focus compared to other groups. To quote from Shih, "a sanctioned ignorance persists regarding how issues of Native American rights, land, and cultural preservation must unsettle the framing and articulation of minority issues."[85] Shih proceeds to make the point that "lest comparative racialization end up displacing yet another marginalized group and constructing yet another implicit hierarchy in a contradiction of insight and blindness, empowerment and disempowerment, it must at each instance be critical of its own assumptions and conclusions."[86] To put it another way, calls to go beyond black and white may very well reinforce another kind of binary, with African Americans and Asian Americans becoming the de facto taken-for-granted frame of comparison.

CRITICAL ETHNIC STUDIES AND COMPARATIVE CRITIQUE

In this article, I have endeavored to provide a reappraisal of the comparative turn in ethnic and race studies through a critical consideration of the scope of Afro-Asian inquiry. I assert that at this critical moment, it is important for Afro-Asian inquiry to think through the challenges and complications of a comparative mode of analysis, to take up the questions that might at once seem far removed, coming from hitherto "extraneous" fields such as black studies and Native American and Indigenous studies. It is important for this body of writing to take up currents and concerns drawing attention to strains of antiblackness undergirding critiques of the black-white binary and claims of the conflation of Indigenous status with the racial minority status of non-Indigenous peoples.

Accordingly, Afro-Asian inquiry stands to profit from a critical engagement with these emergent currents and concerns in a way that fully places questions of power at the center of its political and theoretical inquiry. By the same token, a critical ethnic studies project stands to benefit from a sustained engagement with the aforementioned currents that serve to expand the terrain from which comparative analysis can be undertaken. The challenge is to critically address questions and complications that revolve around the uneven terrain underlying this kind of work, to resist the sort of idealization or facile analogy that has come to mark a significant strand of Afro-Asian inquiry.

ANTONIO T. TIONGSON JR. is assistant professor of American studies at the University of New Mexico. He is author of *Filipinos Represent: DJs, Racial Authenticity, and the Hip-hop Nation* (2013) and coeditor of the anthology *Positively No Filipinos Allowed: Building Communities and Discourse* (2006).

NOTES

1. Colleen Lye, "The Afro-Asian Analogy," *PMLA* 123, no. 5 (October 2008): 1732.

2. Josh Kun and Laura Pulido, eds., *Black and Brown in Los Angeles: Beyond Conflict and Coalition* (Berkeley: University of California Press, 2014), 18.

3. Marta E. Sanchez, *"Shakin' Up" Race and Gender: Intercultural Connections in Puerto Rican, African American, and Chicano Narratives and Culture (1965–1995)* (Austin: University of Texas Press, 2006), 16.

4. See note 2 in the introduction for a list of representative texts.

5. In their mission statement, for example, the Department of Ethnic Studies at the University of California, Berkeley, "encourages the *comparative* study of racialization in the Americas, with a focus on the histories, literatures, and politics of Asian Americans, Chicanos/Latinos, Native American Indians, and African Americans" (emphasis mine). See Department of Ethnic Studies, Mission Statement, University of California, Berkeley, http://ethnicstudies.berkeley.edu/ethnicstudies.php.

6. Helen H. Jun's focus is nineteenth-century black press engagement with Orientalist discourse as a means to grapple with the complications attached to African

American citizenship. See Helen H. Jun, "Black Orientalism: Nineteenth-Century Narratives of Race and U.S. Citizenship," *American Quarterly* 58, no. 4 (2006): 1051.

7. Laura Pulido, *Black, Brown, Yellow, and Left: Radical Activism in Los Angeles* (Berkeley: University of California Press, 2006), 20.

8. Ibid., 21.

9. Andrew F. Jones and Nikhil Pal Singh, "Guest Editors' Introduction," *positions: east asia cultures critique* 11, no. 1 (Spring 2003): 5.

10. Traise Yamamoto, "An Apology to Althea Connor: Private Memory, Public Racialization, and Making a Language," *Journal of Asian American Studies* 5, no. 1 (2002): 15.

11. John D. Márquez, *Black-Brown Solidarity: Racial Politics in the New Gulf South* (Austin: University of Texas Press, 2014).

12. Susan Koshy, "Why the Humanities Matter for Race Studies Today," *PMLA* 123, no. 5 (October 2008): 1547.

13. Ibid., 1548.

14. See Stuart Hall, "New Ethnicities," in *Black British Cultural Studies: A Reader,* ed. Houston A. Baker, Manthia Diawara, and Ruth H. Lindeborg (Chicago: University of Chicago Press, 1996), 163–72. See also Stuart Hall, "What Is This 'Black' in Black Popular Culture," in *Black Popular Culture,* ed. Michelle Wallace and Gina Dent (Seattle: Bay Press, 1992), 21–33.

15. Grace Kyungwon Hong, "Strange Affinities: The Sexual and Gender Politics of Comparative Racialization," *CSW Update Newsletter* (Los Angeles: UCLA Center for the Study of Women, 2007), 7.

16. Ibid.

17. Shu-mei Shih, "Comparative Racialization: An Introduction," *PMLA* 123, no. 5 (October 2008): 1350.

18. Ibid., 1349.

19. Ibid.

20. In particular, Shih draws on Fanon's *Black Skin, White Masks* (New York: Grove Press, 1967) and *The Wretched of the Earth* (New York: Grove Press, 1968).

21. Natalia Molina, *How Race Is Made in America: Immigration, Citizenship, and the Historical Power of Racial Scripts* (Berkeley: University of California Press, 2014), 3.

22. See Michael Omi and Howard Winant, *Racial Formation in the United States: From the 1960s to the 1990s* (New York: Routledge, 1994).

23. David Theo Goldberg, "Racial Comparisons, Relational Racisms: Some Thoughts on Method," *Ethnic and Racial Studies* 32, no. 7 (2009): 1275–76.

24. Ibid., 1275.

25. Ibid., 1279.

26. In a similar vein, Alexander G. Weheliye is wary of comparative approaches because of the way these approaches tend to calcify the nation and re-entrench hierarchies. In Weheliye's view, comparative work presupposes the discreteness of its object of study, fuels competition (for resources, legitimacy, and recognition), and exacerbates tensions among subjugated groups. See Alexander G. Weheliye, *Habeas Viscus: Racializing Assemblages, Biopolitics, and Black Feminist Theories of the Human* (Durham, N.C.: Duke University Press, 2014).

27. Grace Kyungwon Hong and Roderick A. Ferguson, eds., *Strange Affinities: The Gender and Sexual Politics of Comparative Racialization* (Durham, N.C.: Duke University Press, 2011), 1–2.

28. Ibid., 2.

29. Ibid., 16.

30. See, for example, the special issue of *positions* edited by Jones and Singh published in the spring of 2003 and the special issue of *Journal for Asian American Studies* published in February 2002.

31. Fred Ho and Bill V. Mullen, eds., *Afro Asia: Revolutionary Political and Cultural Connections between African Americans and Asian Americans* (Durham, N.C.: Duke University Press, 2008), 1–2.

32. Carolyn Rody, *The Interethnic Imagination: Roots and Passages in Contemporary Asian American Fiction* (New York: Oxford University Press, 2009), 48.

33. Ho and Mullen, *Afro Asia,* 16.

34. Ibid., 2–3.

35. Ibid., 3.

36. Heike Raphael-Hernandez and Shannon Steen, "Introduction," in *AfroAsian Encounters: Culture, History, Politics,* ed. Heike Raphael-Hernandez and Shannon Steen (New York: New York University Press, 2006), 1.

37. Lye, "The Afro-Asian Analogy," 1732.

38. Edward J. W. Park and John S. W. Park, "A New American Dilemma? Asian Americans and Latinos in Race Theorizing," *Journal of Asian American Studies* 2, no. 3 (October 1999): 289–90.

39. Ibid., 305.

40. LeiLani Nishime, "'I'm Blackanese': Buddy-Cop Films, *Rush Hour,* and Asian American and African American Cross-racial Identification," in *Asian North American Identities: Beyond the Hyphen,* ed. Eleanor Ty and Donald C. Goellnicht (Bloomington: Indiana University Press, 2004), 43.

41. Shirley Hune, "An Overview of Asian Pacific American Futures: Shifting Paradigms," in *The State of Asian Pacific America: Policy Issues to the Year 2020* (Los Angeles: Leap Asian Pacific American Public Policy Institute and UCLA Asian American Studies Center, 1993), 5. See also Hune's article "Rethinking Race: Paradigms and Policy Formation," *Amerasia Journal* 21, nos. 1–2 (1995): 29–40.

42. Hune, "Rethinking Race," 31.

43. Michael Omi, "Out of the Melting Pot and into the Fire: Race Relations Policy," in *The State of Asian Pacific America,* 199.

44. Gary Y. Okihiro, *Margins and Mainstreams: Asians in American History and Culture* (Seattle: University of Washington Press, 1994), 33.

45. Ibid., 34.

46. Ibid., 58.

47. Ibid., 62.

48. Also often cited are the works of Vijay Prashad and Bill V. Mullen. Prashad is regularly referenced as providing a frame and piquing interest in the importance of recuperating and reaffirming the buried history of historical, political, and cultural convergences between the two groups. Prashad relies on the notion of polyculturalism to underscore the porousness of culture and the interconnectedness of politics.

He looks to the Bandung Conference as a pivotal moment in terms of cultivating a vision of anticolonial solidarity. Mullen is also an often-cited scholar in this body of work, relying on the notion of Afro-Orientalism to tease out the ways African American and Asian American writers and activists have engaged each other through the prism of Orientalism. Like Prashad, Mullen looks to the Bandung Conference as a consequential moment in terms of serving as an originary moment in the cultivation of Afro-Asian unity. See Vijay Prashad, *Everybody Was Kung Fu Fighting: Afro-Asian Connections and the Myth of Cultural Purity* (Boston: Beacon Press, 2001); and Bill V. Mullen, *Afro-Orientalism* (Minneapolis: University of Minnesota Press, 2004).

49. Amy Abugo Ongiri, "'He Wanted to Be Just like Bruce Lee': African Americans, Kung Fu Theater and Cultural Exchange at the Margins," *Journal of Asian American Studies* 5, no. 1 (February 2002): 31.

50. Nami Kim, "Engaging Afro/black-Orientalism: A Proposal," *Journal of Race, Ethnicity, and Religion* 1, no. 7 (June 2010): 2.

51. Ibid., 13.

52. Vijay Prashad, "Foreword: 'Bandung Is Done'—Passages in AfroAsian Epistemology," in Raphael-Hernandez and Steen, *AfroAsian Encounters*, xiii.

53. Rody, *The Interethnic Imagination*, 48.

54. Ho and Mullen, *Afro Asia*, 5.

55. In the field, Bandung is situated within a larger narrative in which certain figures are referenced for embodying the "spirit" of Bandung. W. E. B. Du Bois, for instance, is an often-cited figure for his embrace of Afro-Asian solidarity, namely how his interest in Asia shaped his political outlook and vision. In particular, Du Bois looked to Asia to work through his anticolonialist vision and politics predicated on a solidarity encompassing the world's majority people of color. Michael T. Martin and Lamont H. Yeakey, for example, underscore how Du Bois's identification with China loomed large in his vision of decolonization. See Michael T. Martin and Lamont H. Yeakey, "Pan-American Asian Solidarity: A Central Theme in DuBois' Conception of Racial Stratification and Struggle," *Phylon* 43, no. 3 (1982): 202–17. For someone like Mullen, a full accounting of Du Bois's political thought and philosophy entails a careful consideration of his musings on Asia, and how Asia always loomed large in his thinking and writing. See Mullen, *Afro-Orientalism*.

56. Najia Aarim-Heriot, *Chinese Immigrants, African Americans, and Racial Anxiety in the United States, 1848–82* (Urbana: University of Illinois Press, 2003).

57. Julia H. Lee, *Interracial Encounters: Reciprocal Representations in African and Asian American Literatures, 1896–1937* (New York: New York University Press, 2011), 3.

58. Ibid., 13–14.

59. Helen Heran Jun, *Race for Citizenship: Black Orientalism and Asian Uplift from Pre-Emancipation to Neoliberal America* (New York: New York University Press, 2011), 149.

60. Ibid., 4.

61. For works along similar lines, see also Eddie Wong, "Comparative Racialization, Immigration Law, and James Williams's *Life and Adventures*," *American*

Literature 84, no. 4 (December 2012): 797–826; and Hsuan L. Hsu, "Sitting in Darkness: Mark Twain and America's Asia," *American Literary History* 25, no. 1 (Spring 2013): 69–84.

62. See, for example, the chapters in Raphael-Hernandez and Steen, *AfroAsian Encounters*.

63. Deborah Elizabeth Whaley, "Black Bodies/Yellow Masks: The Orientalist Aesthetic in Hip-Hop and Black Visual Culture," in *AfroAsian Encounters*, 190.

64. Deborah Wong, "Guest Editor's Introduction: A/A: African American-Asian American Cross-Identifications," *Journal of Asian American Studies* 5, no. 1 (February 2002): 8.

65. Ongiri, "'He Wanted to Be Just like Bruce Lee,'" 39.

66. N. Kim, "Engaging Afro/black-Orientalism," 4.

67. Lye, "The Afro-Asian Analogy," 1735.

68. Yamamoto, "An Apology to Althea Connor," 22.

69. Antoinette Burton, "The Sodalities of Bandung: Toward a Critical 21st-century History," in *Making a World after Empire: The Bandung Moment and Its Political Afterlives*, ed. Christopher J. Lee (Athens: Ohio University Press, 2010), 351.

70. Ibid., 352–53.

71. Lye, "The Afro-Asian Analogy," 1732. Even someone like Prashad, a major figure who espoused Bandung as a highpoint in the actualization of Afro-Asian solidarity, has expressed reservations about the lasting legacy of the conference in terms of establishing solidarity. See his foreword in *AfroAsian Encounters*.

72. Jun, *Race for Citizenship*, 5.

73. Along similar lines, Viet Thanh Nguyen spotlights Asian American studies' investments in and preoccupations with what he describes as "signs of resistance or accommodation" that have served to delimit the field's purview. Specifically, Nguyen is alluding to a tendency within Asian American literary criticism to engage in a certain kind of reading strategy that ultimately serves to flatten Asian American heterogeneity. See Viet Thanh Nguyen, *Race and Resistance: Literature and Politics in Asian America* (New York: Oxford University Press, 2002), 6.

74. Lye, "The Afro-Asian Analogy," 1733.

75. Linda Martín Alcoff, for example, notes that the black/white paradigm privileges a particular form of racial subordination predicated on color, obscuring how racial oppression operates along multiple axes such as nativism. See Linda Martín Alcoff, "Latino/as, Asian Americans, and the Black-White Binary," *The Journal of Ethics* 7, no. 1 (2003): 5–27.

76. Jared Sexton, "Proprieties of Coalition: Blacks, Asians, and the Politics of Policing," *Critical Sociology* 36, no. 1 (2010): 90. See also Sexton's monograph *Amalgamation Schemes: Antiblackness and the Critique of Multiracialism* (Minneapolis: University of Minnesota Press, 2008).

77. Katerina Deliovsky and Tamari Kitossa, "Beyond Black and White: When Going Beyond May Take Us Out of Bounds," *Journal of Black Studies* 44, no. 2 (2013): 173.

78. Janine Young Kim, "Are Asians Black? The Asian-American Civil Rights Agenda and the Contemporary Significance of the Black/White Paradigm," *Yale Law Journal* 108 (1998–99): 2402.

79. Márquez, *Black-Brown Solidarity.*

80. Ibid.

81. Enakshi Dua, "Thinking through Anti-Racism and Indigeneity in Canada," *The Ardent Review* 1, no. 1 (April 2008): 31–35.

82. Park and Park, "A New American Dilemma?"

83. Winona Stevenson, "'Ethnic' Assimilates 'Indigenous': A Study in Intellectual Neocolonialism," *Wicazo Sa Review* 13, no. 1 (Spring 1998): 44.

84. Jodi A. Byrd, *The Transit of Empire: Indigenous Critiques of Colonialism* (Minneapolis: University of Minnesota Press, 2011), xxvi. For a discussion of the problematic deployment of raced frameworks, see also D. Anthony Tyeeme Clark and Norman R. Yetman, "'To Feel the Drumming Earth Come Upward': Indigenizing the American Studies Discipline, Field, Movement," *American Studies* 46, nos. 3/4 (Fall–Winter 2005): 7–21.

85. Shih, "Comparative Racialization," 1351.

86. Ibid., 1351–52.

Precarious Intimacies

Yoko Tawada's Europe

BEVERLY M. WEBER

Behind all images of Europe is the legend of a woman from Asia Minor.
She is abducted, raped, and abandoned. This continent is named after her.
Even today, there are many women living in Europe who have much in
common with Europa. . . . They are here because they thought western
Europe was rich, secure and peaceful, while it creates war, poverty, and
destabilization all over the world. Many of them followed the dream
Europe dreamed about itself: the dream of enlightenment, democracy,
and equality.

"Europe's dream" remains important in two senses: on the one hand
as a democratic, universalistic utopia, on the other as a Eurocentric
nightmare of imperial demands with a long tradition of colonialism
and racism. The antinomies of the European idea continue: oppression
and liberation, nationalism and cosmopolitanism, enlightenment and
regression, universal demands and specific reality go on coexisting. This
indissoluble connection between the European ideal of equality and the
simultaneous reality of unequality [*sic*] is the dream Europe dreams about
itself, and one that can turn into a nightmare at any time.

—Hito Steyerl, "Europe's Dream"

Contemporary discourses of "Europe" exist in a tension between nightmare and dream that the German visual artist and cultural theorist Hito
Steyerl describes in these excerpts from a treatment for her film *Europe's
Dream*. Hope for a just democracy rooted in European Enlightenment projects, and the ongoing realities of violence that continue to mark the lives of
those conceptualized as Other to Europe, produce this tension. The lauded
potential intimacies created by various European projects, but particularly
the European Union—connections between and across internal European
borders, stronger communities rooted in shared economic futures, and re-
newed, even intensified human rights—are constantly haunted by the pasts

and presents of exclusions rooted in racisms, fears of immigrant others, intensified economic insecurity, and the tightening of Europe's external borders. Indeed, the very linkage of human rights, progressive knowledge, and democratic futures to the definition of Europe has paradoxically functioned to produce precarious lives for those deemed Other to Europe.

I open with Steyerl's script here for the perspectives it affords on the dreamworld Europes represented in the prose of Yoko Tawada, a poet, essayist, novelist, and literary critic who lives and works in Germany. The violent intimacy that informs the myth to which Steyerl points—the rape of Europa—is also lived out over and over in the relationships inhabiting Tawada's narratives. Those relationships gesture to the precarity of geographical, historical, and physical intimacies but also to the differing racialized formations of Otherness attached to constructions of "Asia" and "Africa" in order to define "Europe."

What I call here the precarious intimacies of Tawada's work might be thought of as imaginative ways of making legible racializations in Europe as rooted in the violence of Europe's ongoing creation and definition, and refracted through interpersonal intimacies. Many inventions and reinventions of Europe both cover up and produce experiences of economic and legal precarity for those deemed excluded from its definition. Tawada's precarious intimacies invite a practice of reading that gestures to the importance and problems of comparison of racialization when theorizing contemporary imaginations of Europe. The consequences of these processes for the lives of Europe's "Others" can only adequately be apprehended with analytic methods that understand comparison as radically contextualized, and that are cautious to avoid stabilizing, reifying, or essentializing the points of comparison.

I draw here in particular on Tawada's short narrative "The Shadow Man" and her novel *The Naked Eye* as starting points for such considerations. The very differences between these pieces—short and long; one written in Japanese, set in Germany, and translated to English;[1] the other written in Japanese and German, set in East, West, and Unified Germany as well as France, and reworked into German and Japanese-language manuscripts published simultaneously and then translated into English[2]—all point to the asymmetries of comparison itself. My focus here will be the particular asymmetries of gendered and racialized Others within the texts, existing in relationship to contingent, multiple, and shifting formations of Africa, Asia, and Europe. I do not wish to argue that Tawada's work provides an explication of racialization and racisms in Europe. Rather, her imagined Europes invite the reader to consider the contingent, but disjunctive, formations of Asia, Africa, and Europe as well as their ongoing and repeated transformation, leading to the contradictory production of disappearing borders and new borders, and access to new spaces and new confined spaces, overdetermined by histories of colonialism, slavery, fascism, American imperialism, and the Cold War.

INTRODUCING YOKO TAWADA

Yoko Tawada moved from Japan, where she studied Russian literature, to Hamburg in 1982, where she studied German literature. She eventually earned a PhD in German literature. Since 2006, she has lived in Berlin. She writes in a range of genres in both Japanese and German, and has created many texts that have never been translated into the other language, thus eliciting, to some extent, two distinct publics.[3] Tawada's complex work has earned her accolades and awards in both Japanese and German contexts; she has garnered an extensive body of critical attention in Japanese-, German-, and English-speaking contexts as well. She is uniquely situated as an immigrant author who is not expected to "represent" her "originary" national community in the way that many second- and third-generation Turkish German authors are sometimes expected to.[4] Much Tawada scholarship has appropriately focused on the aspects of subjective "becoming" and "in-betweenness" in Tawada's work: the spaces of transit, transition, and translation that celebrate the "becoming" subject.[5] Petra Fachinger shows that the figure of the picaresque in *The Naked Eye* functions to challenge colonialist constructions of ethnicity and race by living in transnational space.[6] However, the construction of intimacies between present and past, between multiple places and spaces, marks not only an undoing and blurring of borders and boundaries but also an evocation of the very existence and re-creation of borders. Tawada's references to Europe, Asia, and Africa point to their ever-changing definitions, but they also point to how reimaginations of Europe nevertheless have created new exclusions. By doing this Tawada's texts move toward making race visible, thus "violat[ing] the powerful narrative of Europe as a colorblind continent, largely untouched by the devastating ideology it exported all over the world."[7]

Tawada's short story "The Shadow Man" (1998) represents violent intimacies produced by the violence of the founding narrative of Europe. One protagonist is based on the historical figure of Anton Wilhelm Amo, the first documented African to attend a German university, who finished a

dissertation in law in 1729 at the university in Halle, and then a dissertation in philosophy in 1734 at the university in Wittenberg. Amo left his post
as professor sometime in the mid-1740s to return to Ghana after being
subjected to increasingly racist campaigns.[8] Tawada's narrative imagines
moments in Amo's personal story from the time of his kidnapping by Dutch
slave traders: as a child, he is sexualized and exoticized by the women who
surround him; as an adult, he falls in love with a Russian woman, who rejects
his advances as a violent threat. Amo's story is juxtaposed in "The Shadow
Man" with the fictional character of Tamao, a late twentieth-century Japanese exchange student who has come to Halle to study the Enlightenment
philosopher and dramaturg Gottfried Ephraim Lessing. Lessing is often
remembered for his friendship with the Jewish German philosopher Moses
Mendelssohn, and for sharing with Mendelssohn advocacy for full Jewish
emancipation. Tamao's internalization of European narratives of white cultural superiority is challenged by another Japanese exchange student, Nana,
who mocks Tamao's simultaneous rejection of and desire for things "Asian."

In Tawada's novel *The Naked Eye* (2004), the Vietnamese protagonist,
who has no consistent name in the text (from here on I will refer to her
as the narrator), journeys from a Cold War East Germany (East Berlin) to
West Germany (Bochum) to France (Paris) and back to reunified Germany
(Bochum); in each city she becomes part of an intimate relationship that
promises freedom but figuratively and literally imprisons her in a domestic
space. The relationship to Jörg is particularly violent: in East Berlin he plies
her with vodka, kidnaps her, and smuggles her across the border while she is
unconscious. After the narrator's escape to Paris for several years, Jörg finds
her again; he drugs her and brings her back to Bochum across a border that
is no longer monitored. Finding herself unable to create a meaningful existence for herself due to her lack of legal status, which prevents her from
enrolling in English classes, finding work, or even obtaining a library card,
the narrator escapes into films starring Catherine Deneuve. She often cannot
understand the words and relies on the images; as she reinvents herself in
dialogue with the imagined plot and characters of the films, she inserts herself anew into deeply misogynist and racist narratives that are embedded
in France's colonial histories. The significance of the narrator's escape into
Deneuve films is underscored by the titling of every chapter after a film.

The intimacies of sexual contact or desire in both *The Naked Eye* and
"The Shadow Man" are marked by and point to the violence enacted in the
creation and definition of Europe. However, I am looking further, to consider how stories, temporalities, and geographies develop attachments to

one another without being fully articulated.[9] These intimacies are related to, but not identical with, those delineated by Lisa Lowe in "The Intimacies of Four Continents." In considering how particular comparative knowledges about imperialism and colonialism have become possible, while others have remained obscured, she points to "global intimacies" from which modern humanism and an accompanying racialized division of labor emerged.[10] Lowe names spatial proximity and adjacent connection (including that produced by the violence of slave trading), privacy (accompanied by a newly distinguished public realm that constructs itself against the sphere of bourgeois intimacy), and the intimacies of contact among colonized subjects that enabled rebellion and resistance. Out of these intimacies a dominant understanding of European Enlightenment and secularism has emerged, a "tradition of liberal philosophy that narrates political emancipation through citizenship in the state, that declares economic freedom in the development of wage labor and an exchange market, and that confers civilization to the human person educated in aesthetic and national culture, in each case universifying particularity, difference, or locality through universal concepts of reason and community."[11] "The Shadow Man" and *The Naked Eye* reveal the impossible access to Enlightenment projects for racialized others: citizenship is denied, access to the labor market is prohibited, and education into a humanist national culture is deemed both necessary and impossible—and thus, entrance into the proper space of "the human" itself is put into question. Tawada's imaginative temporal and spatial intimacies, always linked to physical interpersonal intimacies, invite a practice of reading that will consider the emergence of racializations in conjunction with humanism and Enlightenment projects and their ongoing, but transformed, manifestations and impacts today.

Lauren Berlant, speaking of interpersonal intimacies, argues that intimate attachments raise expectations of a shared narrative that will have particular endings. Yet intimacy's "potential failure to stabilize closeness always haunts its persistent activity."[12] It is this insecure "closeness" and the evocation of specific narratives through intimacy that I wish to highlight here. Tawada's intimacies also lead the reader to expect affinities, similarities, or even solidarities, ones that however perpetually fail. In this way Tawada invites comparisons that call attention to the racializations produced by colonialism, war, and imperialism, even as those comparisons also refuse stable or essentialized relationalities. This marks a departure from much of Tawada's work, which is frequently about living in the "in between," living in imagined border spaces (produced by both geographic and linguistic borders), and through the act of constant and ongoing translation. In "The Shadow Man" and *The Naked Eye,* the potential of "in between" fails; what is highlighted instead is frisson, conflict, disjuncture as borders shift and change.[13]

RACISMS IN "ANOTHER" TIME AND PLACE

Understanding the racializations implicitly evoked in Tawada's writings requires a discussion of the specificities of postwar western European understandings of race. After World War II, a gradual tabooization and consequent exclusion of the word *race* from most mainstream discourses displaced, and continue to displace, racialized signifiers from "race" to "culture" and/or "ethnicity."[14] Especially in the German context, affiliation with "nation" also became especially problematic after the war. Europe often has come to stand in for the nation (inflected by nationalist sentiments) in Germany, but discourses of "European values" circulate throughout other European publics as well. Despite these taboos, words marking race, particularly blackness, and implicitly marking national otherness, have continued to be frequent referents in German popular culture.[15] As Fatima El-Tayeb explains, race is further silenced because it is seen to be something from "outside":

> "Race" thus is both at the center of postwar European identity and doubly invisible: on the one hand, it is associated exclusively with Europe's outside and nonwhite populations, consequently it, and with it the history of colonialism, is externalized and deemed marginal to European identity. On the other hand, the Holocaust and related politics of purity applied to various European populations during the Second World War are central to the continent's self-definition, but are completely "deracialized" (and ultimately as detached from postwar Europe as colonialism). This is how racelessness produces haunting: the ideology represents an active, and never fully successful, attempt to repress race rather than a mere reflection of the latter's absence, thus inevitably depending on violence to assure its success.[16]

This double silence and yet intense presence of racializations also has impacts on research, activism, and policy. One of the most striking manifestations is the often-expressed idea that race and racism are U.S. concepts inappropriate to the European context. One can trace this problem easily, for example, by examining the history of feminist theorizing of intersectionality:

although women of color have been calling for a feminism that attends to the intersections of gender with race and sexuality for decades, intersectionality is seen as a concept that problematically "travels" from the U.S. context and therefore is inadequate for European feminisms (which in turn often deploy intersectionality as a framework while ignoring race).[17]

Racialized groups in Europe are not only produced as outside the nation and outside Europe, but also as from another time. People of color, often but not exclusively through discourses of secularism and human rights, are often located as from cultures lost in the past, or at least, cultures that have not yet "arrived" in the secular, enlightened future:

> This reflects a global discourse of progress and human rights in which the white West invariably claims the lead, maybe not always progressively enough, but certainly always more so than anyone else in this scenario. . . . Racialized queers . . . , like all people of color, are cast as products of a culture that is fundamentally inferior to the secular West, making them necessarily "un-European." This trope can be quickly reinforced because it references well-known clichés perceived as truth, since they align with the overarching binary discourse affirming Europe's status as the center of progress and humanism.[18]

In the German context, this process is currently particularly visible through the racialization of Islam that intensifies after German reunification in 1990, marking Turkish Germans, Germany's largest minoritized population, as part of a nonsecular past. Muslims in Germany thus are seen as outside, as desperately needing to and unable to "integrate" into the progressive present.[19] This relationship is doubled in the European Union's uncomfortable relationship to Turkey, which has sought and been refused entry into the EU repeatedly.[20] Although initially those concerns were framed in terms of economics and modernization, objections later tended to rely on racialized fears of cultural and political difference.[21] Islam has also been racialized throughout Europe, though in different ways depending on national contexts; Muslims serve as a key Other against which Europe is defined. Muslims, and Turkish Germans, are nevertheless remarkably absent (or unmarked) in Tawada's texts. I read this absence as further invitation to recognize the current racialization of European Muslims in relationship to a broad range of other racializations that lead to exclusions from full participation in European publics.

INTIMATE TEMPORALITIES

As Leslie A. Adelson has suggested, Tawada's work (and much contemporary German literature) often proposes a futurity that moves beyond binaries of a destructive past and a utopian future, instead showing parallel intertwined times through time traveler figures.[22] However, a look at these particular texts also suggests that the potential reconfigurations of the relationship between past and future, utopia and dystopia, are also deeply racialized.

Tawada's worlds generate numerous intimate temporalities that reveal and reject the relegation of experiences by people of color in Europe to another time and place. These ways of inhabiting a specific time are made intimate by Tawada's texts, attached to one another by their relationship to histories of slavery, colonialism, and racism. Unlike some of Tawada's other texts, where the figures are interpreted as "time travelers," here times and temporalities are made to touch without a blurring of boundaries; they are jarring, at conflict.

In "Shadow Man," this is accomplished through the juxtapositions of the narratives of Tamao and Amo: the former a fictional character studying Lessing, and the latter based on a historical figure who, it is sometimes claimed (but not within Tawada's text), may have influenced Lessing.[23] Their temporalities are made intimate through the absence of any kind of visible or verbal break between stories in the text. There is nothing, visually, to separate their stories from each other on the page (sometimes not even a paragraph break); close attention to the name being used is the only signal. The similarities between names, and Amo's desire to hide his name, makes this even more difficult. The stories are, however, deeply asymmetrical; Amo's story takes up nearly double the space in the narrative. This seems to be the cause (or effect) of the inherent Europe-centeredness of the text—the only exposure we have to the characters' stories is through their time in Europe. Tawada's attachment of these stories (and their character's temporalities) to one another leads the reader to seek a narrative that can adequately account for the intimacy of these characters and their times.

One might be led through this temporal juxtaposition to consider diverging traditions of the German Enlightenment. Amo's own essays, as imagined in Tawada's narrative, invoke the philosophy of Christian Wolff (the historical figure was known as a Wolffian student and philosopher[24]), but his experiences reflect emerging conceptions of race. The historical Amo's work has been located among several key debates of the time, including discussions of whether the mind can feel or sense; in his work he points out weaknesses in the way in which Descartes discusses the relationship between body and mind, but Amo nevertheless reinforces a central division between body and mind.[25] Tawada's Amo struggles with the notion that pain is a symptom of imperfection in the soul. "The soul does not suffer," writes Amo. "It appears to be in pain when a new connection forms, an invasion takes place, or a collision occurs."[26] As Amo deepens his studies, he is comforted by the idea of a soul that does not feel pain. The omniscient narrator thus attributes the pain Amo experiences in his dreams, which are marked by traumatic memories as well as imaginations of future attacks, as his soul leaving his body. Amo dreams of ships, of moaning men and rotting flesh, of seeing the ships from inside the mouth of a shark, and of being tied up and stabbed with quills. After it dawns on him that his dreams are actually of his time spent on a slave ship after his kidnapping, he is increasingly haunted by the question of what "counts" as human. He is trapped at the collision of a philosophy that seeks to delineate the parameters for human perfection, and the increasing sense that he is not viewed as human in the first place by those around him. It is interesting that the historical Amo's first dissertation, *On the Rights of Moors in Europe*, which argued that slavery and servitude were not compatible with European law, remains absent from Tawada's narrative, which focuses instead on his later writing on sense and feeling. "The Shadow Man" thus reflects the real world disappearance of the manuscript *On the Rights of Moors in Europe*, which is no longer extant, but also gestures to growing assumptions during Amo's lifetime about an "African" temperament unsuited to education into enlightened maturity.

We might recall here that Amo's writing exists in a line of German Enlightenment thinking, in between that of Gottfried Wilhelm von Leibniz and Christian Wolff, and that of Immanuel Kant, whose discussions of peace and human rights emerge in tandem with theorizations of race soon after Amo leaves Germany. While Kant's more developed explications of a theory of race will emerge later, essays in 1764 already anticipate the hierarchy of access to enlightened humanity that Kant will develop, arguing that the "race of the Negroes" can at most be educated into servanthood (but not into reasoned maturity) due to their supposed animated passion and vanity. Kant develops this into a theory of the possibilities for becoming "civilized" that is linked to racialized "characteristics," a theory influenced by ideas emerging from zoology in the day, but also one that will have powerful impact on Western scholarship.[27]

Not yet introduced to a philosophy of reason that will invite access to humanity vis-à-vis the educability and maturity of the subject, and denote

that possibility according to location in a racial hierarchy, Amo nevertheless finds himself confronted with a number of exclusions from the category
of the properly human because of race, gender, and class. These center, in
his mind, around the image of the ship that haunts his memory:[28]

> Herr Petersen said that the goal of philosophy was the moral perfection of
> human beings. Amo, however, didn't have a clear image of what the word
> "human" meant: People said that a human being possessed the ability to
> think. Yet no matter how complex a bird's thoughts might be, it was not
> human. When he asked a fellow student if a scullery maid was human, the
> student sneered and didn't reply. Another student explained with a lewd
> smile that for a human being to be born from a scullery maid's belly, she
> merely needed a human seed to produce the child so that even if the scullery
> maid were a horse she might give birth to a human baby. Amo posed the
> same question to one of his professors. After warning him against getting
> sidetracked by insignificant details, the man advised him to deal logically,
> and severely, with the definition of "human" itself. The question, "Are black
> people on a slave ship human beings?" stayed on the tip of Amo's tongue.[29]

Tawada's story thus imagines a temporal intimacy that attaches forms of
dehumanization that enabled slavery to the later development of Enlightenment thought.

In turn, Amo's story is attached to that of Tamao's. Racializations in
Tamao's time, the late twentieth century, are less clearly reflected and defined
in "The Shadow Man," partly because Tamao himself is unable to articulate
a thought, a position, or a relationship vis-à-vis histories of race. A local
student, Manfred, names Tamao "Amo's descendent," in this way marking
Tamao as racialized Other to both the nation and the field of philosophy;
as Amo's descendent, Tamao is both part of and excluded from Europe.
Tamao, however, doesn't know who that is or what that means. Once he
finds out, he can never forgive Manfred for linking him to Amo.

We might read this in two directions. In the first, Tamao may have so
thoroughly internalized colonial logics exported to Japan from Europe
and the United States that he cannot accept an affinity or closeness to black
subjectivity. In a second reading, Tamao finds himself in a double bind. To
acknowledge an intimacy with Amo would be to acknowledge and reify
Manfred's racialization of Tamao, and therefore to accept an intimacy from
which he cannot speak, excluding him from a position as a subject rather
than object of knowledge. This possibility is reinforced by Tamao's refusal

of Chinese food, fearing that he will become a "mere speck in an Asian throng."[30] Tamao is further disturbed by being seen as a Japanese student, not as a Lessing scholar.[31] The alternative is to deny that intimacy by remaining silent about race, thus reinforcing the contemporary "silence" around race that actually has contributed to new forms of racialization. Thus the bringing together of the times and characters of Tamao and Amo also brings together a diverse set of Enlightenment ideas and thoughts, and a diverse set of racializations in postreunification Germany. Both characters inhabit those times with enforced silences surrounding race, in contexts where explicit theories of race remain yet to be articulated, or part of a supposedly already-dealt-with past.

Tamao's refusal to align himself with histories of racialization in Germany continually leads to an inability to engage with the world around him. Nana, another Japanese exchange student studying Lessing, initially expresses interest in Lessing's most well-known play, *Nathan the Wise* (1779), set in Jerusalem during the Crusades. Tamao can make little sense of this particular Enlightenment project, which is embedded in Lessing's outspoken support for Jewish emancipation as well as a desire to articulate a call for peace via secular reason.[32] Tamao couches his confusion in derision—but he never articulates an alternative research topic of his own; his research topic remains vaguely "Lessing," and only at the behest of his professor at home. When Nana later critiques the gender impacts of seventeenth-century Enlightenment thought, Tamao responds by losing control over his speech, and uttering only meaningless syllables. When Nana later changes her thesis topic to write about Amo instead, Tamao abruptly disappears from the narrative entirely. Tamao's inability to recognize the gendered, racialized history of humanism renders him an ongoing victim of that history, a racialized Asian nonsubject who cannot speak and, ultimately, cannot exist. Amo's own historical participation in a discussion of human rights has thus become literally unimaginable, then juxtaposed with Tamao's inability to imagine an affinity with Amo.

INTIMATE GEOGRAPHIES

In "The Shadow Man," Tawada gestures to the complex histories of racialization through geographical intimacies as well as temporal ones. Geographical intimacies are alluded to initially in a brief reference that relies on a conflation of "Africa" and "Orient" in the minds of scholars, who often discussed peoples from Africa and Asia as "Naturvölker"—literally natural peoples, but meant as "primitive" peoples—as opposed to the "civilized" peoples of Europe, "Kulturvölker."[33] This intimacy is reinforced through the intertwining narratives of a man from Ghana and a man from Japan, who in turn stand in for Africa and Asia. Intimate asymmetrical representations of "Asia" and "Africa," here evoked through the characters of Amo and Tamao, ultimately fail to produce closeness. It is not here that comparison itself fails, but that a failure to compare, or really, to connect, relies on and reifies a postwar silence about race and racialization. Tamao himself dissolves into silence amid his own participation in this silencing. The figure of Nana, alternatively, provides an instance of background secondary doubling in "The Shadow Man"; her implicit gesturing to affinities between forms of racialization highlight Amo's rejection of those intimacies.

Turning to *The Naked Eye,* the use of geographical intimacies to highlight the racialized creation of Europe is even more pronounced. It is difficult to describe the narrator of *The Naked Eye,* or even to clarify whether she exists outside the fantasies of those around her. Like Amo, she is suspicious about speaking her real name, fearing to make herself more vulnerable; unlike Amo, she is a first-person narrator who gives a series of different false names. In the last chapters of the book she projects herself into Catherine Deneuve's films so thoroughly that she is indistinguishable from the film characters. Many anchoring points for the narrator's sense of self have simply disappeared. The narrator's real, and then a forged, passport are lost. The country she first visited in Europe, East Germany, no longer exists; the ideological framework for her own imagination of Vietnam has also disappeared. New temporal intimacies between colonialism, the Cold War, and a post–Cold War era of an integrating Europe are thus represented through the construction of geographical intimacies between France, Germany (East, West, and unified), and Vietnam.

The narrator of *The Naked Eye* is kidnapped twice by a (West) German man named Jörg: first during the Cold War while she is in East Berlin to deliver a speech, and again when he discovers her in France years after the end of the Cold War, at some point after 1998. The narrator becomes in so many ways the myth of Europe, or many of the myths of Europe. She is Europa, kidnapped from Asia (but not Asia Minor), raped, but not abandoned, instead, pursued and hunted in order to be raped and kidnapped again. She functions as a foil for Europe by embodying much that is "not Europe" or "outside to Europe" to the world around her: Communism, Asia, the past, racialized as an exoticized and eroticized passive woman located in a violent heterosexual economy of desire. She fulfills the fantasy of contemporary Europeans, one of the many migrants thought to arrive desperately seeking the rights and freedoms afforded by Europe; one of the many feared migrants who exist at the heart of Europe illegally, unemployed; one of the many feared trafficked from the East. However, the perpetrator is not an Eastern European mafia but a West German man who claims to bring freedom to the East, here doubled in meaning as the east of Vietnam, and East Germany. Although postreunification discourses of race have often located racism in the former East Germany, as if racism has also been conquered in the former West, the violence enacted through Jörg's imagination of the passive Asian woman is not a racism of the East but of the West. In this sense she embodies, but also challenges, many of the contradictory dreams and fears caught up in the imagination of what Europe might become. The dissolving of internal European borders leads to increased trafficking from the East; the intimate connections between an integrating Europe and a globalized world, on the other hand, also result in new borders.

The narrator struggles with the series of lost connections she experiences, leading to the feeling of spaces existing completely isolated from one another. After she has been kidnapped from East Berlin and wakes up in Bochum, she has difficulties imagining where she might be, because everything west of East Germany has been previously unimaginable:

> Despite the distance between them, "here" and "there" had to be connected. The Berlin Wall was said to be more difficult to break through than the Great Wall of China, but on the map of the world in Jörg's room I discovered an unbroken line that reached from Vladivostok to Lisbon. Bochum wasn't on the map. There was no desert in the Western part of Europe. The names of so many different cities were represented that the lines of letters touched.[34]

Here she complements her previous lack of knowledge about Western Europe, the "desert" produced by Cold War politics, with an immediate post–Cold War cliché, "From Vladivostok to Lisbon," meant to call into existence a new European/Eurasian space of economic and cultural cooperation after the Cold War. Despite this new openness, she is trapped in the provincial western German town of Bochum, kidnapped and trapped by her ignorance of how to leave. The presumed promises of a post-Communist Europe remain unfulfilled.

Intimate geographies and their revelation of the violence of Europe are perhaps most clearly explored in *The Naked Eye* through reference to

"Indochina," a space only experienced by the narrator "on the screen in Paris," namely through the 1992 film *Indochine* starring Catherine Deneuve.[35] The chapter titled after this film literally is the center of the book. The name of course refers to the space that the narrator counts as her homeland but cannot recognize as such: "The word sounded like a botched tofu dish. The movie was about neither India nor China—it was about us."[36] Indochina is thus a literal empty center to the book, a colonial construction of Vietnam during the time of anti-imperialist resistance, imagined through an immediate post–Cold War optic that now locates Communism in Asia, reimagined again through the narrator's interpretation of the film images from her childhood perspective as a committed Communist.

The film *Indochine* tells the story of Eliane, often read as representing imperial France, played by Deneuve. Eliane adopts an orphaned Vietnamese princess, Camille. Their relationship is interrupted by Jean-Baptiste, with whom Eliane has an affair, but with whom Camille develops a longer relationship after she wakes up half naked in his arms, mistakenly thinking that he has saved her from an attack. Camille abruptly becomes disillusioned with French imperialism, transforms into a Communist revolutionary, kills a naval officer, and is eventually caught and imprisoned. Deneuve's Eliane, in contrast, renders colonialism palatable, even desirable, in a world where discourses of anti-imperialism have been deemed irrelevant; she provides a nostalgia for the "good times" before French rule "became" violent in response to increasing agitation for independence.[37] Eliane further embodies European civilizing discourse, literally parenting the Vietnamese character into European adulthood. This civilizing mission fails, in part, when her daughter rejects colonial occupation and instead chooses Communist revolution. In Tawada's narrative, the narrator describes the film as a "suitably critical look at the late-stage colonial period that paves the way for revolution," leaving herself open to accusations from her friends that she espouses an outdated Cold War ideology and has forgotten that freedom and independence are French exports. Yet despite the narrator's rejection of imperialist ideologies of French freedom, she identifies strongly with Eliane: when, at the end of the film, Camille yells at Eliane to "go back to France! Indochina is dead!" the narrator feels Eliane, not Camille, "crying within."[38] The narrator repeatedly watches the film, unable to resolve the contradictions between Communist discourses of anti-imperialism and her own identification with Eliane. The film, and the narrator's viewing of it, become a shared experience of a nostalgic closeness that never existed between France and Vietnam. One recalls some of the initial lines of the film spoken by Eliane, not referred to in Tawada's text: "[Camille's parents] had been my dearest friends. . . . We thought the world consisted of inseparable things: men and women, mountains and plains, humans and gods, Indochine and France." The narrator herself seems to engage this nostalgia, though with some discomfort, remembering France as once a "guest" in Vietnam but also remembering her uncle's critique of the nostalgia and desire for things French among upwardly mobile Vietnamese.[39] The imagined intimacy between France and Indochina was embedded in a narrative in which colonialism would lead Vietnam into a European future, yet where the educability of Vietnamese subjects into Europeanness was never really considered possible. This plays out in the narrator's friends' criticism of her viewing of the film: "If only France had been more gentle and adult. . . . But the French administration in Indochina was never as destructive as the Japanese one that preceded it. Besides, we later opposed the Vietnam War. It really might have been possible for Vietnam to develop into an industrial nation in cooperation with us, without Communism or the war."[40] In this way the violence of French colonialism is obscured: it is rendered less dangerous than Japanese colonialism, and replaced in the imagination of the narrator's friends by a paternalistic promise of European freedom.

VIOLENT INTIMACIES, RACIALIZED BODIES

The violence of the relationship between France and Vietnam, offering freedom through European colonialism, echoes the relationship between the narrator and Jörg, who kidnaps the narrator at the beginning and end of *The Naked Eye* to take her to his home in Bochum. When the narrator initially rejects Jörg's proposal to move to Bochum with him, he is astounded, asking, "Don't you want to have freedom?" Once she has been kidnapped and imprisoned in his apartment and bed in Bochum, she fantasizes about stabbing the man who rapes her every night with a long scissors but separates that man from Jörg. She seems strangely detached from her life and at the same time strangely attached to her rapist Jörg, an attachment expressed as loneliness and boredom when he is absent for long stretches. The narrator finally takes action to escape when an angel (later revealed to be Deneuve) stops a train where there is no stop; the narrator assumes this is the train from Paris to Moscow and sneaks aboard. The train instead brings her to Paris. When Jörg finds her in Paris, she does not dismiss him. Instead, she imagines that it is possible that her life with him might be better; the narrator has fully internalized the promise of freedom that will literally be denied her through an intimacy resulting in imprisonment. At the novel's end the narrator wonders of Deneuve, "What freedom did you promise me that night?"

Tawada's work often refracts epistemic, physical, and intimate violence through skin contact. Like the historical Amo, the figure of Amo in "The Shadow Man" is taken from his home and family by Dutch slave traders, one of whom, named only by the Dutch "heer" (lord or master), gives him preferential treatment by bringing him into his room and bed with him. The heer eventually "gifts" Amo to the Duke of Braunschweig in Germany. In the feminized domestic space of the home, the women are obsessed with his skin:

> These females constantly stroked Amo, marveling at the ebony smoothness of his chest. They pinched his buttocks on the sly. The maid whose big, yellow teeth showed when she laughed would grab his penis when no one was looking and not let go. Amo stared at the boy in the mirror as if he were looking at a ghost. Why did he look so different? . . . As he watched the child in the mirror grow prettier each day, Amo thought that no matter where they decided to take him he wouldn't mind as long as he could be with this beautiful boy.[41]

In this passage, Tawada imagines Amo's life in a way that reflects the sexualization and feminization of the African other that formed part of the ideological legitimation for European colonization.[42] Amo's familial intimacies are reduced to a distant contact with the master/father figure, and sexualized abusive contact with most of the women in the household. In adulthood, Amo continues to be exoticized and sexualized in deeply racialized ways. However, he now experiences a new element of deep fear on the part of women, as both his adulthood and the changing discussions of the times expose him to racializations that construct him as a dangerous threat to white bourgeois womanhood and its requisite piety and purity. He is shocked to overhear a conversation between the housemaid and her friends, for example: "They were quizzing Marguerite about what Amo ate, whether his whole body was black, the size of his penis. He was always aware of their eyes, watching him—in the shadow of a fence, behind the trees, from inside their houses. Yet: whenever he approached and tried to speak to them, they looked terrified and ran away."[43] When he falls in love with a woman identified only as "a Russian woman," he agonizes over a letter declaring his love. Trusting nobody else to deliver it, he tries to deliver it himself; caught in the act, he is accused of an attack on the woman and beaten. As rumors circulate about his dangerous sexuality, Amo decides to go to Africa. But the intensified racisms continue after his departure in the form of a satirical drama in which "Amo was a lion who escaped from the jungle, and drooling profusely as he tried to seduce the young lady, she ran away shrieking. A huge tongue drooped wantonly from the lion's mouth like a banana."[44] The experience of dehumanization that accompanied Amo's kidnapping and transport to Europe is thus repeated in his departure from Europe, and a physical, interpersonal intimacy becomes impossible, produced by discourses on race as the violence of a black man in the case of the Russian woman, but experienced by Amo as sexualized abuse by white women in most of his encounters with women. Amo's double, Tamao, is also embedded in violent sexual intimacies, but his are now initiated by himself and realized only in his dreams. A brief episode details a dream rape of Nana, witnessed by Manfred. Within the narrative, this episode serves as further example of Tamao's inability to establish any form of interpersonal intimacy, partly because he imagines those possibilities only within communities he does not wish to be a part of: Japanese students and Lessing scholars.

THE POLITICS AND PROBLEMS OF COMPARISON

What do these temporal and geographical intimacies, expressed via interpersonal violence, mean, then, for considering comparative racializations in relationship to the contemporary transformations of the idea of Europe? I'm suggesting here that Tawada offers up something like a model, perhaps a cautionary tale as well as an invitation, for bringing comparative readings to representations of racialized groups. As I noted earlier, Tawada is not providing a theory of race, racism, or racialization; to the contrary, words derived from "race" are absent in these texts. Yet experiences of racialization are fundamental to her texts' characters and their experiences.

Tawada creates intimacies of narratives, characters, temporalities, and geographies that invite the reader to compare, while also undermining an assumption that this intimacy will necessarily result in closeness, whether we understand that closeness in terms of solidarity, affinities, or similarities. The varied histories of fascism, colonialism, and inventions of race require the problematization of comparison even as they also must be understood as part of the shared heritage of "Europe."[45] Tawada's heterotopic narratives reveal these racializations to be mutually produced, contingent, and yet varied and asymmetrical. The dreamlike movement between times, spaces, and racialized groups does not collapse them into singular narratives but rather highlights the ideological, historical, and geographical ruptures that inform the characters' existence. These narratives of racialization are embedded in the violent memories of fascism, colonialism, and the Cold War, and refracted through the violence of personal intimacy.

The lack of a reference in Tawada's texts to another geographic construction so important to contemporary understandings of Europe, namely that of something like a "Middle East" often understood to be the "Muslim world," is important here. Lowe, in her discussion of possible comparative knowledges of colonialism I referred to earlier, points to the importance of considering the intimacies that link British imperialism and the emigration of Asian laborers to the United States, the intimacies of "four continents" (North America, Asia, Africa, and Europe). "The Shadow Man" and *The Naked Eye* similarly encourage an analytics of comparison that calls attention to related constructions of racialized continents. Tawada implicitly displaces the centrality of the Muslim other via a consideration of the linked production of Asia, Africa, Europe, and the Middle East in contemporary understandings of Europe, similarly "supplement[ing] forgetting with new narratives of affirmation and presence."[46] This allows the reader to locate the racialization of Islam in relationship to the overlapping racializations of Africa and Asia that currently serve to demarcate "Europe." Such a displacement challenges the dominant presumption that the conflicts of the Cold War and colonialism have merely disappeared to be replaced by Islam—instead, they are intimately connected.[47] Destabilizing the terms of this intimacy—Europe, Africa, Asia, Middle East—reveals these connections.

The project of undoing "Europe" (and "Asia" for that matter) informs a large part of Tawada's work available in German or English, as the title of one of her essays, "Really, You Don't Dare to Say It, but Europe Does Not Exist," provocatively suggests. In a rare example of addressing the presence of Islam in Europe, "Is Europe Western?," Tawada points to the problems of assuming that totalitarian ideologies belong to a time and space outside of Europe: "The presenter spoke about a 'Western' political tradition of democracy as if totalitarianism was not part of that tradition." Later she writes: "The term 'Western' . . . tries to wrap up an ideology in a geographic packaging: whoever is in favor of democracy, freedom and individualism is considered Western in their orientation. And, if that person originates from the geographic west then they belong to their own tradition. If not, they have left their own tradition. They may well be modern but they are not completely themselves."[48]

Tawada invites, then, a form of comparison that also recognizes that comparisons, like other forms of knowledge, are embedded in complex histories of the production of race. This recognition is important to a form of comparison pointed to by Shu-mei Shih:

> If racialization is inherently comparative, a psychosocial and historical process, then we are working against the meaning of comparison as the arbitrary juxtaposition of two terms in difference and similarity. . . . [This] form of comparison brings submerged or displaced relationalities into view and reveals these relationalities as the starting point for a fuller understanding of racialization as a comparative process.[49]

Tawada's work asks the reader to consider the relationalities between terms that she imagines together: Europe, Asia, Africa. Yet she does not permit the reader to fall into the trap of using comparison to construct an essentialized understanding of what any of those terms means through an easy evaluation of similarities and differences. Instead, Tawada's texts demand a framework that can more fully address the processes of racialization and their effects by recognizing the precarious nature of the terms of comparison, the attachment of these terms to one another, the instability of those attachments, and therefore the precarity of the very temporalities and geographies that are brought into intimacy in these texts.

BEVERLY M. WEBER is associate professor of German studies at the University of Colorado at Boulder and author of *Violence and Gender in the "New" Europe: Islam in German Culture* (2013).

NOTES

1. The fact that "The Shadow Man" was not published in German seems to have obscured it from research on the text within German studies in North America, and from literary studies in Germany. Tawada surmises that the lack of critical attention to *The Naked Eye* is due to its setting in France. Bettina Brandt, "The Postcommunist Eye: An Interview with Yoko Tawada," *World Literature Today*, no. 1 (2006): 43.

2. Bettina Brandt, "Scattered Leaves: Artist Books and Migration, a Conversation with Yoko Tawada," *Comparative Literature Studies* 45, no. 1 (2008): 12–22. My language abilities afford me access to the German and English texts.

3. Yasemin Yildiz, *Beyond the Mother Tongue: The Postmonolingual Condition* (New York: Fordham University Press, 2012).

4. Leslie A. Adelson, "The Future of Futurity: Alexander Kluge and Yoko Tawada," *The Germanic Review: Literature, Culture, Theory* 86, no. 3 (July 1, 2011): 136.

5. Much of Tawada's writing engages the question of how Europe might be imagined, although the histories of racialization and colonialism are most explicit in the texts I address here. Claudia Breger discusses Tawada's work as deploying strategies of mimicry to reveal Orientalisms. See Claudia Breger, "'Meine Herren, spielt in meinem Gesicht ein Affe?' Strategien der Mimikry in Texten von Emine S. Özdamar und Yoko Tawada," in *AufBrüche: Kulturelle Produktionen von Migrantinnen, Schwarzen und jüdischen Frauen in Deutschland,* ed. Kader Konuk, Peggy Piesche, and Cathy S. Gelbin (Königstein/Taunus: Ulrike Helmer, 1999), 30–59. For discussion of multilingualism, translation, and Tawada's transnational imaginary, see Keijirō Suga, "Translation, Exophony, Omniphony," in *Yoko Tawada: Voices from Everywhere,* ed. Douglas Slaymaker (Plymouth, UK: Lexington Books, 2007), 21–34; Yasemin Yıldız, "Tawada's Multilingual Moves: Towards a Transnational Imaginary," in Slaymaker, *Yoko Tawada: Voices from Everywhere,* 77–90. Tawada is also read as challenging Japanese nationalist, ethnocentric approaches to language; see Reiko Tachibana, "Yoko Tawada's Quest for Exophony: Japan and Germany," in Slaymaker, *Yoko Tawada: Voices from Everywhere,* 153–69.

6. Petra Fachinger, "Postcolonial/Postcommunist Picaresque and the Logic of 'Trans' in Yoko Tawada's *Das nackte Auge,*" in *Yoko Tawada: Poetik der Transformation; Beiträge zum Gesamtwerk; Mit dem Stück "Sancho Pansa" von Yoko Tawada,* ed. Christine Ivanović (Tübingen: Stauffenburg, 2010), 297–328.

7. Fatima El-Tayeb, *European Others: Queering Ethnicity in Postnational Europe* (Minneapolis: University of Minnesota Press, 2011), xv.

8. Scholars speculate that the anticlerical tendencies of his first dissertation in law led to Amo's abrupt departure from the University of Halle (known as an important site for philosophies supporting tolerance and Jewish emancipation) to the University of Wittenberg. William E. Abraham, "Anton Wilhelm Amo," in *A Companion to African Philosophy,* ed. Kwasi Wiredu (Malden, Mass.: Blackwell, 2004), 191–99. Amo also studied medicine and was qualified to advise dissertations in medicine.

9. I am using "articulation" here in the sense often used in cultural studies frameworks, namely to consider how a set of social relations brings together (or forces together) other formations.

10. Lisa Lowe, "The Intimacies of Four Continents," in *Haunted by Empire: Geographies of Intimacy in North American History,* ed. Ann Laura Stoler (Durham, N.C.: Duke University Press, 2006), 191–212.

11. Ibid., 192.

12. Lauren Berlant, "Intimacy: A Special Issue," *Critical Inquiry* 24, no. 2 (January 1, 1998): 282.

13. I will not have space to address this adequately here, but I do wish to call attention to an exception. The narrator's relationship with Marie might be read as a moment when living in the "in between" *does* function in this text, when both intimacy and the nation are queered, and when the narrator enters into a consensual, nonviolent intimacy. Yet even this special space is temporary, unsustainable for the

narrator because she does not want to work as a prostitute and cannot gain legal work. When the narrator leaves this space, she ends up selling her body after all—to medical experimentation—and returns to violent heterosexual relationships.

14. Alana Lentin, "Europe and the Silence about Race," *European Journal of Social Theory* 11, no. 4 (November 1, 2008): 487–503. Of course the precise manifestations of this silence surrounding race varies from country to country, and from region to region, though with similar impacts for people of color: relative exclusion from higher education, limited access to upward mobility, and ongoing experiences of symbolic and physical violence. Alana Lentin's work cited above focuses particularly on the UK context, while the El-Tayeb works cited throughout focus on the Netherlands, France, and Germany. See also Rita Chin and Heide Fehrenbach, "Introduction: What's Race Got to Do with It? Postwar German History in Context," in *After the Nazi Racial State: Difference and Democracy in Germany and Europe*, ed. Rita Chin et al. (Ann Arbor: University of Michigan Press, 2009), 1–29.

15. Fatima El-Tayeb, "Dangerous Liaisons: Race, Nation and German Identity," in *Not So Plain as Black and White: Afro-German Culture and History, 1890–2000*, ed. Patricia Mazon and Reinhild Steingröver (Rochester: University of Rochester Press, 2005), 27–60.

16. El-Tayeb, *European Others*, 6. El-Tayeb draws on Avery Gordon's notion of haunting to think through how race (and as a consequence, racism) are repressed rather than eradicated, to powerful effects. For a critique of the problems of notions of haunting in relationship to Native American studies, see Danika Medak-Saltzman in this issue.

17. Beverly M. Weber, "Gender, Race, Religion, Faith? Rethinking Intersectionality in German Feminisms," *European Journal of Women's Studies* 22, no. 1 (February 2015): 6–7.

18. Fatima El-Tayeb, "Time Travelers and Queer Heterotopias: Narratives from the Muslim Underground," *The Germanic Review: Literature, Culture, Theory* 88, no. 3 (2013): 307.

19. El-Tayeb, *European Others*; El-Tayeb, "Time Travelers and Queer Heterotopias"; Beverly M. Weber, *Violence and Gender in the "New" Europe* (New York: Palgrave Macmillan, 2013), 77–113.

20. Ziya Onis, "Turkey, Europe and the Paradoxes of Identity," *Mediterranean Quarterly* 10, no. 3 (1999): 135–36.

21. El-Tayeb, *European Others*, 106–7, 115–16.

22. Leslie A. Adelson, "The Future of Futurity: Alexander Kluge and Yoko Tawada," *The Germanic Review: Literature, Culture, Theory* 86, no. 3 (July 1, 2011): 153–84.

23. Margaret Mitsutani, "Translator's Afterword," in Yoko Tawada, *Facing the Bridge*, trans. Margaret Mitsutani (New York: New Directions, 2007), 178.

24. May Opitz, Katharina Oguntoye, and Dagmar Schulz, *Showing Our Colors: Afro-German Women Speak Out* (Amherst: University of Massachusetts Press, 1992), 4.

25. Abraham, "Anton Wilhelm Amo," especially 195–99; see also Kwasi Wiredu, "Amo's Critique of Descartes' Philosophy of Mind," in Wiredu, *A Companion to African Philosophy*, 200–206.

26. Yoko Tawada, "The Shadow Man," in Tawada, *Facing the Bridge,* 32.

27. Peggy Piesche, "Der 'Fortschritt' Der Aufklärung—Kants 'Race' Und Die Zentrierung Des Weißen Subjekts," in *Mythen, Masken Und Subjekte: Kritische Weissseinsforschung in Deutschland,* ed. Maureen Maisha Eggers et al. (Münster: Unrast, 2005), 14–17. There is extensive debate about the consequence of Kant's racism for his philosophical legacy, such as those discussed in Sara Eigen and Mark Joseph Larrimore, eds., *The German Invention of Race* (Albany: State University of New York Press, 2012). A particularly productive engagement occurs in Gayatri Chakravorty Spivak, *An Aesthetic Education in the Era of Globalization* (Cambridge, Mass.: Harvard University Press, 2012), in which she argues for a strategy of using Kant against Kant, or as she terms it, an ab-use of Kant.

28. Tawada, "The Shadow Man," 20.

29. Ibid., 28.

30. Ibid., 30.

31. Ibid., 29.

32. As with all calls for "toleration" vis-à-vis religious others, the play risks replicating processes of othering even as it condemns anti-Semitism and anti-Islamic sentiment. See, for example, Ritchie Robertson, *The "Jewish Question" in German Literature, 1749–1939: Emancipation and Its Discontents* (New York: Oxford University Press, 1999), 38–45. For an extended critique of the notion of tolerance as it emerges in conjunction with colonialism and imperialism, see Wendy Brown, *Regulating Aversion: Tolerance in the Age of Identity and Empire* (Princeton, N.J.: Princeton University Press, 2008).

33. Tawada, "The Shadow Man," 36.

34. Yoko Tawada, *The Naked Eye,* trans. Susan Bernofsky (New York: New Directions, 2009), 30.

35. Ibid., 98.

36. Ibid., 105.

37. Alison Murray, "Women, Nostalgia, Memory: Chocolat, Outremer, and Indochine," *Research in African Literatures* 33, no. 2 (2002): 235–44.

38. Tawada, *The Naked Eye,* 111–14.

39. Ibid., 13.

40. Ibid., 105–6.

41. Tawada, "The Shadow Man," 7–8.

42. Opitz, Oguntoye, and Schultz, *Showing Our Colors;* see also Anne McClintock, *Imperial Leather: Race, Gender, and Sexuality in the Colonial Contest* (New York: Routledge, 1995).

43. Tawada, "The Shadow Man," 43.

44. Ibid., 47–48.

45. Shu-mei Shih, "Comparative Racialization: An Introduction," *PMLA* 123, no. 5 (October 1, 2008): 1349–52.

46. Lowe, "The Intimacies of Four Continents," 207.

47. Brandt, "The Postcommunist Eye," 45.

48. Yoko Tawada, "Is Europe Western?," *Kyoto Journal,* September 20, 2005, http://www.kyotojournal.org/the-journal/kj-classics/is-europe-western/.

49. Shih, "Comparative Racialization," 1353.

"Little More than Desert Wasteland"

Race, Development, and Settler Colonialism in the Mexicali Valley

GEORGE LUNA-PEÑA

In the early 1920s, the Institute of Social and Religious Research at Stanford University funded a project to investigate the economic, educational, social, religious, and civic conditions among "Chinese, Japanese, and other non-European residents of the Pacific Coast of the United States and Canada."[1] The survey, which was first directed by the economist Eliot G. Mears and later the well-known sociologist Robert E. Park, sought to gather life histories up and down the Pacific coast in order to illuminate race relations in the early twentieth century.[2] By the mid-1920s, when the project was considering expanding into Mexico and Hawai'i, researchers crossed the Mexico-U.S. border and interviewed H. H. Clark, the General Manager of the Colorado River Land Company (CRLC)—an American corporation based in Los Angeles that owned over 850,000 acres of land in the Mexicali Valley.[3]

The majority of Clark's short interview focused on the operational specifics of managing a significantly high percentage of the arable land in the Mexicali Valley: water levels, the best type of cotton seed, drainage systems, yearly production, price per bale, and so forth. Yet Clark's interview was framed by two comments that provide a contemporary reader with a more complex view of the Mexicali Valley. At the beginning of his interview, Clark states, "Chinese began to come in to the Mexicali region in 1902. At one time, there was as high as 8000 Chinese employed on our ranch." Then, at the end, Clark speculates about the future of the CRLC's land holdings in the Mexicali Valley: "We do not expect to hold this land permanently, but want to divide it up and sell it out eventually to Scandinavians or Italians."[4] These two comments, which bookend Clark's interview, seem almost nonchalantly expressed. Yet I suggest they unwittingly carry with them the weight of histories of the Mexicali Valley both written about and forgotten, or, to be frank, purposefully erased.

For one, Clark's mention of the Chinese speaks directly to a history of racialized labor in the Mexicali Valley that is important for this article.[5] This specific history, and the history of Chinese in northern Mexico more generally, is one that has been explored by a number of scholars on both sides of the Mexico-U.S. border, including Evelyn Hu-DeHart, Robert Chao Romero, and Grace Peña Delgado.[6] Many of them mention the large Chinese population imported to work and inhabit the land at the beginning of the twentieth century, the often-poor working conditions the Chinese encountered, and the anti-Chinese sentiment that swept across much of northern Mexico during 1920s and 1930s. A majority of these studies seem content with pointing out what, in a different context, Helen Heran Jun calls "proof of second-class citizenship," as if that alone can serve to represent the fullness, complexity, and contradictions of the Chinese experience in Mexico.[7]

What all these scholars overlook, deny, or forget, however, and what Clark's second comment alludes to through its own more direct performance of denial and erasure, is a history of the Mexicali Valley that takes the continued presence of Indigenous peoples seriously, if this is considered at all. When Clark states that the CRLC does not "expect to hold [its] land permanently," he is by no means suggesting it will somehow be returned back to the Cucapá tribe that has inhabited the area for centuries.[8] Instead, Clark follows up his assertion by stating that they will likely parcel the land and sell it to "Scandinavians or Italians." In failing to mention or recognize the Indigenous presence/present in the Mexicali Valley, Clark continues a pattern of erasure that is common in other settler colonial contexts.[9]

Unlike previous studies that have approached the peoples that inhabited the Mexicali Valley during this time period in an almost compartmentalized fashion, this article instead seeks to focus its attention on the relationship the Chinese and the Cucapá were essentially placed into. This analysis is offered in an attempt "to situate these different histories in complex unity," to borrow Dean Saranillio's words, but to do so in a way that does not overdetermine the products of this relationship.[10] In other words, if we understand both the Chinese and the Cucapá to have been oppressed by the structures and systems that dramatically reshaped daily life in the Mexicali Valley during the first three decades of the twentieth century, then we must also recognize that it would be a mistake to presume they were oppressed in the same manner or fought that oppression in ways that exemplify "multiracial solidarity."[11] Instead, this article begins to shed light on a more complex relationship—one that was absolutely configured through the influence of the settler colonial context in which it was lived out.

To do so, it becomes necessary to rethink the Mexicali Valley in four different but definitely connected ways. First, I argue against the historiography of the Mexicali Valley that often presents this space as a barren wasteland, or Mexico's northern frontier of "unoccupied lands."[12] Here, Mexican state policies and scholarly studies on both sides of the border plainly ignore the presence of Indigenous peoples and their relationship to land. Second, I argue that the celebratory rehashing of the development of the Mexicali Valley by scholars normalizes the exploitation of racialized Chinese labor and the dispossession/displacement of Indigenous peoples and lands in the area. Rather than name this "development" for what it is—settler colonialism and settler capitalism—studies have instead presented this story as one of progress and improvement. Next, I argue that what María Josefina Saldaña-Portillo has identified as the "success of *mestizaje* as a racial ideology" has, until now, contributed to the disinclination to engage the Mexicali Valley in the manner it should be: as a settler colonial space.[13] In other words, *mestizaje* serves as part of what Andrea Smith refers to as "the normalizing logics of settler colonialism."[14] I suggest, then, that only by grappling with *mestizaje*—the biological and cultural blending or mixing of Indigenous, Spanish, and African peoples in Latin America—we can begin to recognize how recuperative and de/anti-colonial projects can also serve to buttress colonial ideologies that Clark's comments about land ownership, usage, and futures represent. Finally, recognizing the Mexicali Valley as a settler colonial space implicates Chinese immigrants to the region as settlers. I make this conceptual move in order to argue, as Smith reminds us, that the "capitalist conception of land forces all people who migrate (whether it be through enslavement, migration, or relocation) to become 'settlers'" and also to point out that Chinese "success" in the area—what has often been historicized as a celebratory story of racial progress—has been "paved over Native lands and sovereignty" and must, then, be accountable in the present to Indigenous peoples.[15]

BACKWARD, SCANTILY POPULATED, AND IN NEED OF DEVELOPMENT

The Mexicali Valley sits on the northeast corner of northern Baja California, bordering the U.S. states of California and Arizona as well as the Mexican state of Sonora. For decades before the Colorado River Land Company took possession of over 850,000 acres of land in the valley, Mexican officials attempted, without much success, a series of "colonization plans" meant to entice European immigration to the area. President Porfirio Díaz's brand of liberalism, for example, which commanded the Mexican political land-scape from 1876 through 1911, was characterized by a push to attract foreign investment, an effort to enact liberal immigration laws, and an anxious desire to spur capitalist economic development especially in the northern parts of the country.[16] However, previous administrations traversed similar paths. For example, the administrations of Ignacio Comonfort, Benito Juárez, and Sebastián Lerdo de Tejado—all, like Díaz, from Mexico's Partido Liberal (Liberal Party)—attempted to attract foreign, namely European, investment and immigration to the Baja California area through various surveying and colonization schemes.[17]

What all these administrations blatantly disregarded, which subsequent scholarly studies of the area have discursively perpetuated, was the fact that the lands of northern Baja California were already inhabited by various Indigenous tribes. The Mexicali Valley alone, for example, was the ancestral home of the Cucapá, Kiliwa, Pai Pai, and Kumiai.[18] This disregard for Indig-enous peoples seems to be premised on a belief that the Indigenous rep-resents "an outmoded and dead way of life [and] an anachronistic mode of production."[19] The *científicos,* for example, a group of men that served as Porfirio Díaz's "brain trust," believed that Indigenous peoples were "the bane of Mexico," and that their way of living could "hardly be entrusted" with modernizing a country.[20] Indigenous relationships to land and use of resources, then, were seen as contrary to the imperatives of stimulating the development of the northern parts of the country, to building a "modern, industrial society."[21] In this way, Mexican officials came to see European immigration as the answer to their frustrations over the assumption that Indigenous peoples would slow attempts toward progress and modernity. Justo Sierra, for example, a trusted Porfirian *científico* and avid Social Dar-winist, shared a common *científico* belief when he claimed that "only Euro-pean blood can keep the level of civilization . . . from sinking."[22] Here, Sierra links "European blood" to a seemingly innate ability to increase the level of a civilization. By extension, Sierra also suggests that without "Europeans" to build this modern and industrial society, this "civilized" blood will be diluted by "savage" blood—a logic of colonialism that discursively constructs Euro-peans as more deserving of these lands than Indigenous peoples.

This discursive production of undeserving Indigenous peoples also plays itself out in the pages of hundreds of scholarly texts on the history of the

Mexicali Valley. Here, I would like to turn our attention to one in particular: U.S. historian Dorothy Pierson Kerig's "Yankee Enclave: The Colorado River Land Company and Mexican Agrarian Reform in Baja California, 1902–1944." Written in the late 1980s, Kerig's "Yankee Enclave" study was the first to have extensive access to the CRLC's archives, so it has become well known and oft quoted among scholars of the Mexicali Valley—by those interested in agriculture, foreign capital in the region, and water issues—and even scholars of the Chinese in Mexico. Additionally, it was translated into and published in Spanish by the Universidad Autónoma de Baja California in the early 2000s under the title *El valle de Mexicali y la Colorado River Land Company, 1902–1946*, a fact that underscores its significance to a broad audience.[23] In fact, in the prologue to the Spanish translation, the Mexican scholar Aidé Grijalva wrote that Kerig's study was "foundational for future studies on the historical background of present day Mexicali Valley."[24]

Kerig's "Yankee Enclave" seeks to recuperate a history of the Mexicali Valley through the eyes and archives of the Colorado River Land Company in order to highlight what she describes as the "positive role that the Colorado River Land Company played, during a crucial time period in Mexico's modern development."[25] In other words, for Kerig, previous studies of the Mexicali Valley, particularly those produced by Mexican scholars, often cast the CRLC as a "villain" or focused too much on the company's "negative aspects."[26] In contrast, Kerig seeks to give credit to the CRLC for what she sees as the positive and important contributions the company made to the Mexicali Valley for more than four decades.

"Yankee Enclave" begins with a chapter titled "Prelude to Development," which paints a picture of the Mexicali Valley as "little more than an arid wasteland." Kerig goes through great discursive pains to characterize the Mexicali Valley as an ignored area of Mexico ("distant and isolated") that is neither modern nor well populated ("backward and scantily populated") but also holds immense agricultural promise ("potentially productive land").[27] In the process of setting the stage for the CRLC to be presented as the triumphant savior of the Mexicali Valley, Kerig severely diminishes both the presence and significance of Indigenous peoples in the area and their relationship to these lands. In effect, she presents the Mexicali Valley as "an emptied space open to settler claims of belonging" and ownership.[28] Kerig does not completely ignore Indigenous presence. Her strategy, instead, like that of the *científicos* before her, is to downplay their significance and essentially argue that Mexico's future as a modern industrial nation could not be guaranteed by relying on the labor and industry of the presumed inferior

Indigenous peoples. In other words, and to borrow from Jodi A. Byrd, Kerig depicts Indigenous peoples as "past tense presences . . . [who] remain as lamentable casualties of national progress."[29]

For example, Kerig writes that the "primitive native population did not engage in agriculture, except in rudimentary form along the Colorado River delta." She continues on to state that the "aborigines lived simply and sparsely—often close to starvation."[30] Here, Kerig presents the Indigenous peoples of the Mexicali Valley as basically unable to take care of themselves, ignoring the fact that they lived and survived in what she had deemed an "arid wasteland" for centuries. It should be noted, however, that the Cucapá, although focused on fishing for much of their sustenance, did grow beans, squash, maize, melons, and other fruits and vegetables by taking advantage of the natural irrigation the overflow from the Colorado River often provided. This agricultural system was a sophisticated method of farming on arid lands, tied to an intimate knowledge of the land and that made canals and pipes unnecessary. Kerig, however, ignores this and instead discursively presents the Indigenous peoples of the Mexicali Valley as "backward" and premodern and in dire need of rescue, lest they soon starve to death. She follows, then, a long line of scholars that have utilized the trope of the "disappearing native" as a discursive strategy to normalize and naturalize the eventual possession of Indigenous lands by settlers. In other words, describing Indigenous peoples and their agricultural techniques as "primitive" and "rudimentary" diminishes the significance of their presence and also serves to justify dispossessing Indigenous peoples of their lands since they were not making it "productive." Kerig's "Yankee Enclave," then, presents Indigenous peoples as having no viable place in the future of the region.

A second and related discursive strategy Kerig employs is the celebratory rhetoric of development. After characterizing the Mexicali Valley as an unproductive and backward wasteland—"an isolated, neglected, and impoverished Mexican federal territory with few inhabitants"—she then introduces the Colorado River Land Company as the catalyst of the area's development and transformation: "Its metamorphosis [the Mexicali Valley's] was set into motion, shortly after the turn of the century, with the introduction by the Colorado River Land Company of large-scale, irrigated, commercial agriculture." The result, for Kerig, was that the CRLC "greatly enhanced the economic value" of these lands and helped make the Mexicali Valley the "thriving urban, commercial, industrial, and administrative center that it is today."[31]

For Kerig, the story of development in the Mexicali Valley is one of extensive lateral canals, irrigation ditches, rows of commercial agricultural crops (especially cotton), agreements on water rights, railroad tracks for transporting goods to markets, and so forth. In short, development is about making "improvements" to the land so it ceases being potentially productive and starts being actually productive. Production here, of course, is measured by economic profits. But what Kerig completely ignores is that the story of the Mexicali Valley's development into the "thriving" area it is today is not one of a benevolent American corporation but instead one premised on the dispossession of Indigenous land and the exploitation of racialized labor, in particular Chinese labor. This history, then, is similar to the one that Manu Vimalassery has outlined in the U.S. territory of Nevada, where "racialized labor sustained and expanded the production of capital" and simultaneously "sustained and expanded colonialism" over Indigenous lives and land.[32] Yet Kerig glosses over this with a celebratory history of development that paints the Colorado River Land Company as a heroic savior: of the Mexicali Valley, of Mexico, of Indigenous peoples, and of the Chinese.

If we are to reconceptualize the space of the Mexicali Valley as a space of settler colonialism, as this article will iron out in the coming pages, then avoiding the celebratory rhetoric of the area's development, coming to terms with the dispossession of Indigenous lands, and asserting an Indigenous presence/present are good places to start. I turn briefly to the arrival of the Chinese in the Mexicali Valley before turning to questions of settler colonialism in the area.

CHINESE IN BIG LUSONG

A small number of what Grace Peña Delgado has dubbed "Chinese *fronterizos*" had already begun to settle in the northern part of Baja California during the late nineteenth century.[33] Many scholars attribute this to the fact that the Chinese Exclusion Act of 1882 in the United States had prohibited Chinese immigration, thus a small community of Chinese decided to settle just south of the Mexico-U.S. border. Although at first hesitant because European immigration was preferable, Mexico's president Porfirio Díaz on June 3, 1900, signed the Treaty of Amity, Commerce, and Navigation with the Chinese government, which, as one scholar wrote, "opened wide the floodgates of Chinese immigration to Mexico as it allowed for 'free and voluntary' movement between the two countries."[34] Within ten years of the treaty being signed, the Chinese population in Mexico rose by over 1,000 percent from a community of 1,023 to one of over 13,000 people. In that same time period, every state in Mexico, except for the central state Tlax-cala, could boast that it had a Chinese community.[35]

Yet the northern region of the country—namely Sonora and the territory of Baja California—received more Chinese immigrants than any other part of the country. In 1926, for example, nearly one-quarter (24 percent) of the Chinese population in Mexico was situated in Baja California alone.[36] Robert Chao Romero speculates this is the case because Baja California "offered both direct access to U.S. territory and abundant employment and commercial opportunities."[37] In the Mexicali Valley, some scholars estimate the Chinese community made up over 40 percent of the region's population.[38] An overwhelmingly large majority of the Chinese population in the Mexicali Valley worked on the lands owned and leased by the Colorado River Land Company.

The CRLC's policy with the land it purchased was to lease large chunks of it out to foreign commercial growers. This was, of course, a strategic move on the part of the CRLC because it helped to entrench the corporation's legal ownership of the land and protect its title from adverse claims. "Every bona fide lessee," explains Kerig, "had to sign a rental contract that, by its very nature, acknowledged the company as the rightful landowner."[39] We see, then, the ways settler capitalism reconceptualizes and reconfigures land in the name of economic profit.

Thousands of Chinese nationals migrated to the Mexicali Valley in search of work in the fields. They found work picking cotton in the commercial agricultural fields owned by the CRLC, and eventually, hundreds of them were able to rent or lease their own lands from the company—with, of course, a portion of their profits being transferred to the CRLC.[40] John Dwyer points out that many of the Chinese that had leased lands in the Mexicali Valley "organized cooperative societies that only employed Asian workers. A few of the wealthier Chinese lessees imported workers from China."[41] As was made clear by H. H. Clark, at one point there were over eight thousand Chinese working the lands that the CRLC had purchased in the Mexicali Valley. In other words, the Chinese were a significant community in the Mexicali Valley—the largest immigrant group in the region—and contributed to making it one of the "world's largest cotton-producing regions" during this time.[42]

However, the Chinese also transitioned from working in the fields of the Mexicali Valley to working in and eventually owning many shops in

Mexicali. A considerable number of Chinese "transitioned into employment as merchants involved in the grocery and dry goods trade" and achieved an even higher degree of economic success. In fact, Chao Romero writes, "Chinese shops were ubiquitous and dotted the streets and neighborhoods of Sonora, Chihuahua, and Baja California."[43] There is, for example, the story of the Chong brothers—Jose, Cuy, and Lung—who invested in and eventually owned the Las Quince Letras Company in Mexicali, which sold groceries, Chinese herbs, and dry goods.[44] While the Chinese had become a large part of the reason for the Mexicali Valley's agricultural success, they also contributed to its commercial success.

This upward economic mobility, some scholars have argued, is what, in part, fueled an intense anti-Chinese movement in northern Mexico during the 1920s and 1930s. The epicenter of this anti-Chinese movement was in Sonora where, in 1931, anti-miscegenation legislation barred Chinese men and Mexican women from marrying.[45] Anti-Chinese sentiment also stretched out into the Mexicali Valley, where similar disdain for perceived Chinese success was expressed. Chinese immigrants in Baja California were "physically attacked, verbally insulted, and exhorted for money by their Mexican neighbors."[46] In the early 1930s, the Partido Nacionalista Pro-Raza was formed in Mexicali with a primary goal of lobbying Baja California's government to segregate Chinese merchants into separate areas of the city.[47] Anti-Chinese sentiment and rhetoric was so bad in Mexicali that one union that represented mostly Mexican service workers claimed that "the Chinese . . . compete with us with bars, grocery stores, meat markets, laundries, 'tortilla' factories. . . . All the commercial life in the territory . . . is in the hands of the everlasting yellow octopus, who continues to suck Mexican workers' blood."[48] In this statement, the Chinese are described with racial imagery ("the everlasting yellow octopus") that portrays them as a parasitic population, corrupting and exploiting the Mexican nation and its workers, literally sucking the "Mexican workers' blood." Not only, then, is this a matter of labor competition, but as this sentiment shows, there is also a profound anxiety about the Mexican nation's racial make-up and future. So much so, in fact, that "[by] 1932, there were 215 anti-Chinese clubs in Mexico boasting a membership of almost 2 million people."[49]

The racial difference the Chinese represented for Mexico and Mexicans is evident, of course, in the anti-miscegenation legislation passed in northern Mexico, but also in the discourse of local politicians. José María Dávila, Baja California's federal congressional representative, for example, argued that the Chinese should be forced to leave Mexico because "they do not represent a step forward in the ideal mestizaje . . . but rather signify a step backwards in the anthropological search for the prototypical man."[50] For Dávila, like many in Mexico after the revolution, the ideal of *mestizaje* signified the mixing of Indigenous and European blood to produce the "modern mestizo national."[51] In this equation, the subject of the mestizo represents both a past and a future. The discourse of *mestizaje* celebrates Indigeneity as "an abstract cultural value from the past" while simultaneously presenting the Europeanized mestizo subject as "a model for Mexico's future."[52] What we see, then, in the mestizo subject is what Taunya Lovell Banks has described as a "movement toward whiteness," where whiteness is assumed to guarantee a collective future for Mexico.[53] In the vision of that collective, Europeanized mestizo future, Chao Romero reminds us that the "Chinese represented a threat to Mexican *mestizaje* and the development of a unified national racial identity."[54]

I will discuss *mestizaje* more in the next section; however, I would like to also keep in mind the complexity of the situation. In other words, although the Chinese faced their own exploitation and discrimination in northern Mexico, their labor and capital also helped to continue the dispossession of Cucapá peoples and lands. This is a part of the history that no scholars of the Mexicali Valley have discussed or explored, including scholars who specifically focus their attention on the Chinese in northern Mexico. To be clear, in pointing this out, I do not mean to minimize the material violence that Chinese so often faced or to argue that although the Chinese faced these very negative and violent backlashes, the Cucapá of the Mexicali Valley fared far worse. Instead, I see this as a reality of the Mexicali Valley during this time period—one that deserves to be pointed out if we are to rethink the area as a settler colonial space.

SETTLER COLONIALISM, ASIAN SETTLER COLONIALISM, AND *MESTIZAJE* IN THE MEXICALI VALLEY

This section draws on the work of settler colonialism studies and Asian settler colonialism to reconceptualize the Mexicali Valley as a settler colonial space. Over the past fifteen years, settler colonialism has begun to receive attention within Asian American studies in the form of Asian settler colonialism, namely in Hawai'i. This section, then, engages with and expands the discussion surrounding Asian settler colonialism by shifting its geographic focus to the Mexicali Valley. In doing so, I address both the discussion around the usefulness of a white settler colonial paradigm for a specific

Latin American context—in this case, the Mexicali Valley—and that uniquely Latin American racial ideology known as *mestizaje*.[55]

In her essay "'How Many Mexicans [Is] a Horse Worth?': The League of United Latin American Citizens, Desegregation Cases, and Chicano Historiography," which was published in a special issue of the *South Atlantic Quarterly* on settler colonialism, María Josefina Saldaña-Portillo attempts to understand the reasons why studies of white settler colonialism, despite their "vast geographic scope," their global reach, have failed to manifest in a Latin American context.[56] Frustrated, Saldaña-Portillo suggests

> that the lack of attention to Spain's colonial practices in the Americas is due less to historical differences than to the success of *mestizaje* as a racial ideology. It is precisely the embrace—within and beyond Latin America—of *mestizaje* as an all-encompassing racial reality that places it beyond historical interrogation, outside the paradigm of white settler colonialism because it did not produce the dichotomous racial formations we see in the United States or South Africa.[57]

Saldaña-Portillo's article is primarily interested in fleshing out the ways in which Mexican Americans made sense of what she calls "two profoundly distinct racial ideologies"—*mestizaje* on the one hand, and the black-white racial binary of the United States on the other.[58] Saldaña-Portillo makes it very clear that making a definitive decision about whether a white settler colonialism model fits the Latin American context is outside the scope of her article. She is not interested, in other words, in the Indigenous populations of Latin America for this particular piece but instead in the Mexican-origin population of the U.S. Southwest.[59] The main questions that she posits, for example, speak to this: "what of the Mexicans . . . white settlers encountered in the newly annexed 'Southwest'? How were they perceived racially? And, more important, how did they perceive themselves?"[60] With this in mind, Saldaña-Portillo goes on to explicate the strategies and thinking embedded within two desegregation court cases argued by the League of United Latin American Citizens (LULAC) in the mid-twentieth century, and critiques a certain strand of Chicana/o historiographic responses to the arguments presented in those court cases.

Despite its focus on the U.S. Southwest, however, Saldaña-Portillo's article is useful in helping to determine whether a white settler colonialism paradigm, and by extension Asian settler colonialism, is adequate for beginning to describe the situation in the Mexicali Valley. Again, Saldaña-Portillo identifies the racial ideology of *mestizaje,* and its success, as part of the reason that Latin America has received little attention in the field of settler colonial studies. But I do not understand her to be arguing that a white settler colonialism paradigm is not adequate for a Latin American context, only that it has certain limits that need to be further worked out.

I understand settler colonialism to be primarily interested in dominating and expropriating land, and as Patrick Wolfe reminds us, a settler colonial invasion is "a structure not an event."[61] Its power, Maile Arvin has argued, stems from multiple means: economic ("the turning of land and natural resources into profit"), ideological ("culturally and morally defined ways of being and knowing resulting from European and post-Enlightenment thoughts"), and juridical ("the imposition of the legal-political apparatus of a settler nation-state, rather than an Indigenous form of governance").[62] However, Arvin also reminds us that each one of these settler colonial forms of power need not be present in order to understand settler colonialism as operative in a particular space. In the Hawaiian context, for example, Arvin recalls that the "economic and ideological components of settler colonialism preceded its legal-political expression, as Christian missionaries and plantation owners and operators (often missionary descendants) worked within the existing legal-political structures of the Hawaiian monarchy until it no longer adequately suited their needs."[63]

I see a similar situation in the Mexicali Valley. My decision to characterize this region as a settler colonial space has a lot to do with the economic and ideological forms of settler colonial power that were present there. Economically ("the turning of land and natural resources into profit"), we have already seen the existence of an American-based corporation whose sole mission was to "develop" the lands of the Mexicali Valley—the ancestral lands of the Cucapá—so that they could yield the highest profit possible.[64] I will not rehash this story here. Instead, I will focus on the ideological structure of settler colonial power that I see present in the Mexicali Valley: *mestizaje.*

Ultimately, I suggest that the "success of *mestizaje* as a racial ideology"— which again, Saldaña-Portillo argues has helped place "it beyond historical interrogation, outside the paradigm of white settler colonialism"—is due to the fact that it is itself a form of settler colonial power.[65] In other words, the purpose of *mestizaje* as an ideology and a reality in much of Latin America is to serve the settler colonial goal of dominating Indigenous land.

Countless scholars have critiqued *mestizaje,* in particular, for what we could call the celebratory embrace of it in certain critical fields of study. For example, Nicole M. Guidotti-Hernández argues that the "politics that center around celebrating or reclaiming *mestizaje* are highly problematic because of what they elide from the colonial past and nationalist present."[66] For Guidotti-Hernández, what an embrace of *mestizaje* helps to occlude is the very real racialized and gendered violence of the Mexico-U.S. borderlands. Guidotti-Hernández also critiques Chicano studies discourses around *mestizaje* for their fetishization of an "Indian essence" built upon uninterrogated assumptions about Indigeneity, which, as she points out, ultimately serves as a form of epistemic violence.[67] Likewise, Saldaña-Portillo, in her brilliant book *The Revolutionary Imagination in the Americas and the Age of Development*, argues that "we can no longer uncritically celebrate mestizaje in Chicana/o and other social formations as a positionality of radical, postmodern hybridity but must recognize it as a racial ideology with its own developmentalist history."[68]

The work that the settler colonial ideology of *mestizaje* does—and let us be clear here that it does this work in the service of the Mexican nation-state, a nation-state that historically has been and is presently opposed, at times violently, to Indigenous sovereignty, forms of governance, and relationships to land—is "developmentalist" in the sense that it "posits Indian difference as an originary moment in the formation of national consciousness to be superseded by mestizo universality."[69] In other words, the ideology of *mestizaje* positions Indigenous subjectivity as something to be overcome while simultaneously imbuing mestizo subjectivity—more specifically a Europeanized mestizo subjectivity—with futurity. In the formula of *mestizaje*, "racial mixture is evoked as the future."[70] The triumph of *mestizaje*, then, is the mestizo, and the triumph of the mestizo is whiteness, or a white future.[71] Whiteness is what emerges "from behind the mask of Indian difference" and what ultimately gives the mestizo "access to the promises of modernity in his future."[72] In short, *mestizaje* has been a formidable ideological tool of settler colonialism, deployed to conceal the continued existence of Indigenous peoples—like the Cucapá in the Mexicali Valley—and their claims to sovereignty.

If the Mexicali Valley is a settler colonial space—based on the economic and ideological structures of settler colonial power present there—then what do we make of the large Chinese community that still calls the Mexicali Valley home today?[73] I would argue, like previous scholars have argued in other geographic regions—namely Hawai'i—that the concept of Asian settler colonialism helps us make sense of the Chinese/Cucapá relationship. In the context of Hawai'i, Candace Fujikane has described Asian settler colonialism

as the "constellation of the colonial ideologies and practices of Asian settlers who currently support the broader structure of the U.S. settler state."[74]
Using a similar definition, then, I would suggest that the Chinese who have
called the Mexicali Valley home are indeed settlers. Their historical and
continued presence in the Mexicali Valley has served to carry on the goals
of the settler colonial structures of power that help constitute the area. I
characterize the Chinese community in Mexicali as settlers not necessarily
to pass blame for the continued dispossession of Indigenous lands on them
specifically but more so to bring to the fore what Fujikane has described as
"the responsibilities that Asian settlers have in supporting Native peoples in
their struggles for self-determination."[75]

Arguing that *mestizaje*—as an ideological tool of settler colonialism—
reinforces whiteness and naturalizes settler claims to Indigenous lands begs
the question: how, then, are the Chinese in the Mexicali Valley complicit or
implicated within the context of a settler colonial order in relation to Indigenous peoples notwithstanding their marginalized status and an ideology—
mestizaje—that seeks to disavow their participation in the narrative of the
nation? To answer this question, I turn our attention to the specific claims
made by Asian settlers to the Mexicali Valley. In doing so, it is important to
keep in mind that power, or settler colonial power, "does not simply target
historically oppressed communities but also operates through their practices, ambitions, narratives, and silences."[76]

On January 27, 1937, a group of four hundred *agraristas*—Mexican farm
workers, many of whom had migrated to the Mexicali Valley from different
parts of the country—met in Colonia Michoacán de Ocampo and com-
menced a seizure of portions of the Colorado River Land Company's holdings.[77] This event, which gained national attention at the time and has since
become immortalized as El Asalto a las Tierras ("the attack on the lands"),
triggered then President Lázaro Cárdenas to begin the process of expropriating most of the CRLC's irrigated land holdings for "redistribution to
Mexican field workers as communal *ejidos*."[78]

During this takeover, the *agraristas* forced out tenants who had been
leasing land from the CRLC. Many of these tenants where Chinese, but this
group also consisted of other settlers—Japanese, Germans, Italians, and
more-well-off Mexican nationals. Almost immediately, Chinese and other
tenants formed an association to lobby federal and state agencies and repre-
sentatives to help protect the lands they had leased. As John Dwyer reminds
us, "those who lost their land in the Mexicali Valley did not accept the
expropriation without contest."[79]

In fact, the Chinese and other lessees made some very specific rhetorical claims that are evidence of their complicity in the settler colonial structures of power present in the Mexicali Valley. Many of the Chinese lessees considered themselves independent farmers and were not interested in the *ejido* system—communal lands split into smaller parcels that are farmed by individual community members.[80] To stake claims to the land, and to hopefully gather support and protection for those claims, the Chinese and other tenants employed the rhetoric of being "local" and questioned the "authenticity" of the "outsider" *agraristas,* whom, they pointed out, had only recently migrated to the area.[81] They cited their "long-term roots" in the Mexicali Valley and made reference to themselves as "traditional" campesinos as strategies to lobby for protection of the lands they leased from the CRLC.[82] The strategy of claiming a "local" identity is one that we see in the Asian settler colonial context of Hawai'i as well. There, the reference to being "local" is used to "establish a problematic claim" to Indigenous lands.[83] "Local," in the Hawaiian context, Haunani-Kay Trask reminds us, "is, itself, a particularly celebrated American gloss for 'settler.'"[84]

In addition, the Chinese and other tenants made specific references to their relationship to the land via the "improvements" they had made, thus trying to position themselves as deserving of those lands, and, by extension, the Cucapá as undeserving. In letters to federal officials, for example, Chinese and other lessees wrote about the canals and irrigation systems that they had installed on the lands they leased. They also made reference to their "great efforts and sacrifice" in the Mexicali Valley.[85] In effect, the tenants of the CRLC's lands were arguing that their contributions were significant to the development of the region. But this narrative and rhetorical strategy also serves to naturalize and even celebrate the "process of expropriating territories and the elimination of Indigenous modes of production." Put differently, in claiming their role in the Mexicali Valley's "development," Chinese immigrants necessarily position themselves as more deserving of the land than Indigenous peoples and against the assumed, "uncultivated place it was prior to their arrival."[86] Here, then, Indigenous relationships to land, modes of production, and use of resources are all relegated to the status of expendable. This rhetorical strategy is similar to what Bianca Isaki has called a "sentimental aggression," which she describes as "a 'loving the land' that can come to contest Indigenous claims to territory."[87] In other words, settlers have "loved" the land by improving it, at times through great sacrifice, and these sentiments are presented as the evidence of their presumed entitlement to Indigenous lands.

The narratives of belonging (being "local") and deserving (because of the "improvements" they have made to the land) the Chinese rely on in the Mexicali Valley not only help them make specific claims to Indigenous lands in the area but also help them navigate the racial ideology of *mestizaje*—which, as we have seen, seeks to exclude them. In other words, if the ideal of the Europeanized mestizo subject is premised on a "movement toward whiteness,"[88] then Chinese claims to Indigenous lands are themselves a move toward whiteness. "In settler colonial contexts," Arvin reminds us, "whiteness is an 'ascendant' ideology, folding peoples into it, encouraging peoples to identify with the power/knowledge of whiteness even when they are individually excluded from identifying as white."[89] Put differently, if in a settler colonial context whiteness is naturalized as deserving of land and equated with possession of land, then for the Chinese in the Mexicali Valley to make a claim to that land means that they are, in effect, claiming whiteness *through* land. It is the possession and improvement of that land that allows the Chinese in the Mexicali Valley to see and position themselves as part of the Mexican nation-state. Claiming whiteness through land, then, helps the Chinese manage the limitations that *mestizaje* sets on them.

This article has paid attention to the Mexicali Valley as a space where the "transformative process of settler occupation" continues to operate through economic and ideological structures of power and where the Indigenous peoples of this area "continue to live under the conditions of this occupation, its disavowal, and its ongoing life."[90] Rather than perpetuate the narrative of the Mexicali Valley as a barren "wasteland" ripe for development by American corporations, as other scholars have done, this article has instead attempted to rethink the Mexicali Valley as a space with a history not often told, to consider "a preceding moment in time, a different arrangement of land, resources and a way of life that predates the settler state."[91] In other words, to be responsible to the Indigenous present, we must continue to bring to the fore Indigenous presence. If we hesitate to point out those responsibilities, then, as Candace Fujikane following Haunani-Kay Trask reminds us, this "makes possible the historical fantasy of settler states evolving into 'multicultural nations.'"[92] This article has also argued that the ideology of *mestizaje* today serves to keep together that "historical fantasy." However, continuing to point out settler responsibilities to Indigenous peoples is one strategy to start to dismantle its illusions. I have discussed the Chinese in the Mexicali Valley in relation to the Cucapá not as a form or ritual of passing blame but instead as a way to help us "[open] our eyes to how power works and how we can redirect it so that it doesn't diminish us all."[93]

GEORGE LUNA-PEÑA works at Generation Justice, a multimedia movement in Albuquerque, New Mexico, training youth to harness the power of media and give rise to narratives that inspire social change.

NOTES

1. "A Register of the Survey of Race Relation records," Online Archive of California, http://www.oac.cdlib.org/findaid/ark:/13030/tf2q2n98s9/entire_text/.

2. The interviews were to be published in a series of volumes edited by Robert E. Park. Only one volume, edited by Eliot G. Mears, actually materialized ("Tentative Findings of the Survey of Race Relations") because the project ran out of funding.

3. In order to "sidestep federal laws that prohibited foreign land-ownership near the border," the CRLC was actually incorporated as a Mexican corporation, but its headquarters—and the place where major decisions were made—was in Los Angeles. The owners of the CRLC were all American businessmen: Harry Chandler, George Hunt, William Allen, Otto Brant, and Oliver Clark also owned the Title Insurance and Trust Company in California and Harrison Gray Otis was the owner and publisher of the *Los Angeles Times*. John J. Dwyer, *The Agrarian Dispute: The Expropriation of American-Owned Rural Land in Postrevolutionary Mexico* (Durham, N.C.: Duke University Press, 2008), 31–32.

4. "Interview with H. H. Clark, manager of Colorado River Land Company, Mexicali Mexico," Survey of Race Relations records, Hoover Institution Archives, http://collections.stanford.edu/pdf/10100000000026_0006.pdf.

5. To be clear, the Chinese were not the only immigrant group that migrated into the Mexicali Valley. There were also Japanese, Germans, and Italians, just to name a few. However, the Chinese were the largest immigrant group in the area.

6. Evelyn Hu-DeHart, "Immigrants to a Developing Society: The Chinese in Northern Mexico, 1873–1932," *Journal of Arizona History* 21 (1980): 49–86; Robert Chao Romero, *The Chinese in Mexico, 1882–1940* (Tucson: University of Arizona Press, 2010); Grace Peña Delgado, *Making the Chinese Mexican: Global Migration, Localism, and Exclusion in the U.S.-Mexico Borderlands* (Palo Alto: Stanford University Press, 2013). For more on the Chinese in Mexico, see Kif Augustine-Adams, "Making Mexico: Legal Nationality, Chinese Race, and the 1930 Population Census," *Law and History Review* 27, no. 1 (2009): 113–44; Charles C. Cumberland, "The Sonora Chinese and the Mexican Revolution," *Hispanic American Historical Review* 40 (1960): 191–211; Philip A. Dennis, "The Anti-Chinese Campaigns in Sonora, Mexico," *Ethnohistory* 26, no. 1 (1979): 65–80; Maricela González-Félix, *El proceso de aculturación de la población de origen chino en la ciudad de Mexicali* (Mexicali: Universidad Autónoma de Baja California, 1990); Catalina V. Morales, *Los inmigrantes chinos en Baja California, 1920–1937* (Mexicali: Universidad Autónoma de Baja California, 2001); José Luis Trueba Lara, *Los chinos en Sonora: Una historia olvidada* (Hermosillo: Instituto de Investigaciones Históricas, 1990).

7. Helen Heran Jun, *Race for Citizenship: Black Orientalism and Asian Uplift from Pre-Emancipation to Neoliberal America* (New York: New York University Press, 2011), 2.

8. The Mexicali region is the ancestral home of the Cucapá, Kiliwa, Pai Pai, and Kumiai. However, for the purposes of this article I will focus on the Cucapá since theirs was the land that was purchased by the CRLC. As José Alfredo Gómez Estrada points out, "Sólo los cucapá vivieron en un territorio con potencial agrícola." José Alfredo Gómez Estrada, *La gente del delta Río Colorado Indígenas, colonizadores, y ejidatarios* (Mexicali: Universidad Autónoma de Baja California, 2000), 113.

9. As Patrick Wolfe reminds us, "Settler colonialism destroys to replace." Patrick Wolfe, "Settler Colonialism and the Elimination of the Native," *Journal of Genocide Research* 8, no. 4 (2006): 388. To say a bit more on erasure, just over one hundred miles west of the Mexicali Valley is the city of Tijuana. Here, Heriberto Yépez reminds us of the "cover-up of the real etymology of Tijuana." Despite the fact that the name most likely derives from the Yumana word for "dry land" *(yanti-juan)*, there is an active and what Yépez calls an "idiotic legend" that the name of the city came from a woman named Tía Juana who owned a large ranch in the area during the nineteenth century. For Yépez, this myth is evidence that "we prefer to erase all of the indigenous symbols from the sign." Heriberto Yépez, "Tijuanalogies: An Urban Essay," in *Tijuana Dreaming: Life and Art at the Global Border,* ed. Josh Kun and Fiamma Montezemolo (Durham, N.C.: Duke University Press, 2012), 51.

10. Dean Saranillio, "Why Asian Settler Colonialism Matters: A Thought Piece on Critiques, Debates, and Indigenous Difference," *Settler Colonial Studies* 3, nos. 3–4 (2013): 282.

11. Jun, *Race for Citizenship*, 4.

12. Dorothy Pierson Kerig, "Yankee Enclave: The Colorado River Land Company and Mexican Agrarian Reform in Baja California, 1902–1944" (PhD diss., University of California at Irvine, 1988), 30.

13. María Josefina Saldaña-Portillo, "'How Many Mexicans [Is] a Horse Worth?': The League of United Latin American Citizens, Desegregation Cases, and Chicano Historiography," *South Atlantic Quarterly* 107 (2008): 812.

14. Andrea Smith, "Queer Theory and Native Studies: The Heteronormativity of Settler Colonialism," *GLQ: A Journal of Lesbian and Gay Studies* 16, nos. 1–2 (2010): 42.

15. Andrea Smith, "Indigeneity, Settler Colonialism, White Supremacy," in *Racial Formation in the Twenty-First Century*, ed. Daniel Martinez HoSang, Oneka LaBennett, and Laura Pulido (Berkeley: University of California Press, 2012), 83; Saranillio, "Why Asian Settler Colonialism Matters," 286.

16. Peña Delgado, *Making the Chinese Mexican*, 9.

17. In 1856, for example, the government of Ignacio Comonfort contracted a Swiss-owned company to survey and map the "public lands" of Baja California, Sonora, and the isthmus of Tehuantepec. The Swiss company, as payment, was to receive one-third of the area it surveyed. Less than ten years later, the administration of Benito Juárez, as a colonization concession, granted a group of San Francisco–based entrepreneurs roughly two-thirds of the Baja California peninsula. And ten years after that, Lerdo de Tejada's government passed a law that authorized land concessions in exchange for surveying and mapping services, much like the contract

that Comonfort had provided the Swiss-owned company twenty years before. Kerig, "Yankee Enclave," 21–22.

18. Gómez Estrada, *La gente del delta*, 113.

19. Saranillio, "Why Asian Settler Colonialism Matters," 289.

20. Peña Delgado, *Making Chinese Mexican*, 31.

21. Ibid.

22. Ibid.

23. Dorothy Pierson Kerig, *El valle de Mexicali y la Colorado River Land Company, 1902–1946* (Mexicali: Universidad Autónoma de Baja California, 2001).

24. Aidé Grijalva, "Prólogo," in Kerig, *El valle de Mexicali*, 13 (translations mine).

25. Kerig, "Yankee Enclave," 11–12.

26. Ibid., 9. It should be noted, as well, that many of the studies that take a more critical look at the Colorado River Land Company still fail to elaborate its responsibility for the dispossession of Indigenous lands in the Mexicali Valley. Pablo Herrera Carrillo, *Colonización del Valle de Mexicali, B.C.* (Mexicali: Compañia Mexicana de Terrenos de Río Colorado, 1958); Pablo L. Martínez, *Historia de Baja California* (Mexico City: Libros Mexicanos, 1956); Edna Aidé Grijalva Larrañaga, "La Colorado River Land Company," in *Panorama histórico de Baja California*, ed. David Piñera Ramírez (Tijuana: Investigaciones Históricas UABC, 1983), 350–61.

27. Kerig, "Yankee Enclave," 42, 20, 36, 3.

28. Bianca Isaki, "HB 645, Settler Sexuality, and the Politics of Local Asian Domesticity in Hawai'i," *Settler Colonial Studies* 1, no. 2 (2011): 86.

29. Jodi A. Byrd, *Transit of Empire: Indigenous Critiques of Colonialism* (Minneapolis: University of Minnesota Press, 2011), xx.

30. Kerig, "Yankee Enclave," 32–33.

31. Ibid., 16.

32. Manu Vimalassery, "The Prose of Counter-Sovereignty," in *Formations of United States Colonialism*, ed. Alyosha Goldstein (Durham, N.C.: Duke University Press, 2014), 89.

33. Peña Delgado, *Making the Chinese Mexican*, 5. Lusong is a district in the Hunan province in China. The Chinese referred to Mexico as Big Lusong and to the Philippines as Little Lusong.

34. Chao Romero, *The Chinese in Mexico*, 27.

35. Ibid., 29.

36. Ibid., 63.

37. Ibid., 57.

38. Dwyer, *The Agrarian Dispute*, 33.

39. Kerig, "Yankee Enclave," 105.

40. For more on the transnational economic networks that the Chinese were a part of, which oftentimes allowed them to pool their resources together to lease land, see Chao Romero, *The Chinese in Mexico*, 30–65.

41. Dwyer, *The Agrarian Dispute*, 97.

42. Ibid., 33. At one point, the lands owned by the CRLC were making $18 million annually through its sale of cotton worldwide.

43. Chao Romero, *The Chinese in Mexico*, 1–2.

44. Ibid., 48.

45. For more on the anti-miscegenation laws in Sonora, see Chao Romero, *The Chinese in Mexico*, 145–90.

46. Dwyer, *The Agrarian Dispute*, 96.

47. Ibid.

48. Quoted in Dwyer, *The Agrarian Dispute*, 98.

49. Elliot Young, *Alien Nation: Chinese Migration in the Americas from the Coolie Era through World War II* (Chapel Hill: University of North Carolina Press, 2014), 220.

50. Ibid., 96.

51. María Josefina Saldaña-Portillo, *The Revolutionary Imagination in the Americas and the Age of Development* (Durham, N.C.: Duke University Press, 2003), 196.

52. Dwyer, *The Agrarian Dispute*, 94.

53. Taunya Lovell Banks, "*Mestizaje* and the Mexican *Mestizo* Self: *No Hay Sangre Negra*, So There Is No Blackness," *Southern California Interdisciplinary Law Journal* 15, no. 2 (2006): 231.

54. Chao Romero, *The Chinese in Mexico*, 89.

55. I would like to be clear first, however, that I am not interested in making generalized statements about the whole of Mexico, and certainly not the entirety of Latin America. Instead, I am interested in the specificity of the Mexicali Valley. Although I realize that my decision to characterize the area as a settler colonial space may have implications for other Latin American contexts, the arguments I present here should be taken solely as arising from, and therefore applying to, the Mexicali Valley.

56. Saldaña-Portillo, "'How Many Mexicans [Is] a Horse Worth?,'" 811.

57. Ibid., 812.

58. Ibid.

59. Insofar as she is more interested in the U.S. Southwest and the Mexican-origin community of this region, Saldaña-Portillo's article has much in common with Rosaura Sánchez and Beatrice Pita's recent article "Rethinking Settler Colonialism," where they critique comparisons of settler colonialism in Palestine and the Chicana/o U.S. Southwest. Ultimately, they argue that to apply a settler colonial paradigm to the U.S. Southwest via its Chicana/o population is mistaken. Rosaura Sánchez and Beatrice Pita, "Rethinking Settler Colonialism," *American Quarterly* 66, no. 4 (2014): 1039–55.

60. Saldaña-Portillo, "'How Many Mexicans [Is] a Horse Worth?,'" 812.

61. Patrick Wolfe, *Settler Colonialism and the Transformation of Anthropology: The Politics and Poetics of an Ethnographic Event* (London: Cassell, 1999), 2.

62. Maile Arvin, "Pacifically Possessed: Scientific Production and Native Hawaiian Critique of the 'Almost White' Polynesian Race" (PhD diss., University of California at San Diego, 2013), 9.

63. Ibid., 10.

64. The CRLC was not the only foreign company that "owned" land in the Mexicali Valley. Altogether, foreign companies owned over 90 percent of the land in the valley, but the CRLC, by far, possessed the most amount of land.

65. Saldaña-Portillo, "'How Many Mexicans [Is] a Horse Worth?,'" 812.

66. Nicole M. Guidotti-Hernández, *Unspeakable Violence: Remapping U.S. and Mexican National Imagineries* (Durham, N.C.: Duke University Press, 2011), 19.

67. Ibid., 17–18.

68. Saldaña-Portillo, *The Revolutionary Imagination*, 12.

69. Ibid., 225.

70. Guidotti-Hernández, *Unspeakable Violence*, 17.

71. Although this short article does not provide the space, there is a lot too that can be said about *mestizaje*'s antiblack origins.

72. Saldaña-Portillo, *The Revolutionary Imagination*, 253.

73. Today, Mexicali still boasts one of the largest Chinese communities in Mexico as well as the largest Chinatown, La Chinesa.

74. Candace Fujikane, "Introduction: Asian Settler Colonialism in the U.S. Colony of Hawai'i," in *Asian Settler Colonialism: From Local Governance to the Habits of Everyday Life in Hawai'i*, ed. Candace Fujikane and Jonathan Y. Okamura (Honolulu: University of Hawai'i Press, 2008), 6.

75. Ibid., 7.

76. Saranillio, "Why Asian Settler Colonialism Matters," 288.

77. Dwyer, *The Agrarian Dispute*, 70.

78. Kerig, "Yankee Enclave," 2. Less than ten years later, the CRLC would cease operations in the Mexicali Valley.

79. Dwyer, *The Agrarian Dispute*, 69.

80. Ibid.

81. Ibid., 70.

82. Ibid.

83. Fujikane, "Introduction: Asian Settler Colonialism in the U.S. Colony of Hawai'i," 6.

84. Haunani-Kay Trask, "Settlers of Color and 'Immigrant' Hegemony: 'Locals' in Hawai'i," in *Asian Settler Colonialism: From Local Governance to the Habits of Everyday Life in Hawai'i*, ed. Candace Fujikane and Jonathan Y. Okamura (Honolulu: University of Hawai'i Press, 2008), 46.

85. Dwyer, *The Agrarian Dispute*, 70.

86. Saranillio, "Why Asian Settler Colonialism Matters," 289.

87. Isaki, "HB 645," 83.

88. Lovell Banks, "*Mestizaje* and the Mexican *Mestizo* Self," 231.

89. Arvin, "Pacifically Possessed," 22.

90. Audra Simpson, *Mohawk Interruptus: Political Life across the Borders of Settler States* (Durham, N.C.: Duke University Press, 2014), 2.

91. Saranillio, "Why Asian Settler Colonialism Matters," 290.

92. Fujikane, "Introduction: Asian Settler Colonialism in the U.S. Colony of Hawai'i," 11.

93. Shona N. Jackson, *Creole Indigeneity: Between Myth and Nation in the Caribbean* (Minneapolis: University of Minnesota Press, 2012), 38.

Being or Nothingness

Indigeneity, Antiblackness, and Settler Colonial Critique

IYKO DAY

his special issue's focus on comparative racial scholarship gives me an
opportunity to weigh in on the specific interplay of race and settler colonialism within an expanding sphere of American studies, one that intersects
with and broadens the long-standing critical terrain of Indigenous studies
in North America. I am particularly interested in exploring the connection
between settler colonial studies and black studies, especially in relation to
binary formulations of colonial and racial formation. This is expressed either
as an Indigenous/settler binary constituted in relation to land or a black/
nonblack binary founded on racial slavery. These approaches are at times
deeply skeptical of relational or comparative analyses of race and reject any
coalitional premise that unifies people of color generally. On this count,
Jared Sexton argues that a form of "people-of-color-blindness" is embedded
in the relational concept of "people of color," one that fundamentally mis-
understands "the specificity of antiblackness and presumes or insists upon
the monolithic character of victimization under white supremacy."[1] Acknowledging these points, I focus on the exceptionalism produced by these binary
frameworks, whereby both the Native and the black body signify a genocidal
limit concept. For instance, Patrick Wolfe casts settler colonialism as a zero-
sum game that requires "the elimination of Native alternatives" and results
in the "social death of Nativeness."[2] Alternatively, writing from the perspective of Afro-pessimism, Frank B. Wilderson III writes, "from the very beginning, we [black people] were meant to be accumulated and die."[3] Extending
an Afro-pessimist critique to the field of settler colonial American studies,
moreover, Sexton argues that settler colonial decolonization movements for
Indigenous sovereignty embrace a Negrophobic discourse of "post-racialism
by diminishing or denying the significance of race in thinking about the
relative structural positions of black and non-black populations."[4] To be
clear, my intentions in this article are not to engage in an evaluation of who

the greater victim is—even if this kind of evaluation is precisely the objective of the scholarship under discussion. Rather, it is to probe the discursive construction of colonial and racial exceptionalism itself, particularly in terms of their relation to a privileged conception of labor within Karl Marx's theory of primitive accumulation. For it is within these chapters of *Capital, Volume I* that Marx connects enslavement and colonial genocide under a broader logic of capitalist accumulation through the violent expropriation of land and labor. Guiding this inquiry is a larger motivating question about whether settler colonial critique has an immanent capacity to examine race.

Before I proceed, I want to acknowledge that the intersection of Indigeneity and antiblackness in the continental United States presents a unique set of issues, insofar as Occupied Palestine and Hawai'i have emerged as equally if not more prominent than the continental United States as sites for theorizing the eliminatory logics of settler colonialism.[5] Part of this centrifugal dynamic may be attributed to the fact that unlike other white settler colonies like Canada, where colonial dispossession is the paradigmatic signifier of white settler supremacy, in the continental United States it has been the legacy of slavery and antiblack racism. This is certainly not to say that the ongoing dispossession of Indigenous peoples in the United States goes completely unacknowledged but rather to appreciate the fact that alongside recent Indigenous sovereignty movements such as Idle No More in Canada or the BDS movement in Occupied Palestine, it has been Ferguson in the United States. Thus, the centrifugal or long-distance lens that I associate with settler colonial *American* studies is clearly a reflection of the continued tensions around theorizing the intersection of race and Indigeneity. Together with what Saidiya Hartman calls the "afterlife of slavery," the logic of antiblackness complicates a settler colonial binary framed around a central Indigenous/settler opposition.[6] Understandably, there is conceptual difficulty in folding the experience of racial capture and enslavement into the subject position of the "settler."

But if we move outside the continental United States, questions raised by such binaries dissipate in the face of the starkest and most brutal binary colonial formations. Occupied Palestine, a comparatively recent site of settler colonialism, is such a place, powerfully magnifying the struggle between settler and Indigenous populations in ways that recall the frontier violence of nineteenth-century America. The illegal occupation, siege of Gaza, and ongoing construction of residential settlements on the West Bank is an uncanny corollary to the lead up to the 1830 Indian Removal Act, which relocated tens of thousands of peoples from the Southeastern Nations east of the Mississippi River. From this view, the glaring binarism of Occupied Palestine offers a window onto U.S. history. But it is for the same reason that Bill V. Mullen's description of Occupied Palestine as "the most dialectical place on Earth" is unable to capture the racial heterogeneity of the continental United States in the present tense.[7] Further, in the case of Hawai'i, another relatively recent site of settler colonialism, Asian Americans have replaced original white settlers and transformed and extended those eliminatory logics into a formation of Asian settler colonialism that is also reflective of the Indigenous/settler binary.[8] As Dean Saranillio explains, "While migration in and of itself does not equate to colonialism, migration to a settler colonial space, where Native lands and resources are under political, ecological, and spiritual contestation, means the political agency of immigrant communities can bolster a colonial system initiated by White settlers."[9] The lesson that Hawai'i offers is one in which a formerly exploited migrant population has achieved structural dominance. Although white settlers exploited indentured Asian laborers in the 1890s as part of the process of dispossessing Native Hawaiians of their land, Asian American invocations of "local" identity and rejection of Native Hawaiian claims for sovereignty reproduce the logics of colonial dispossession. Here Patrick Wolfe's clarification that settler colonialism is a "structure not an event" is especially salient.[10]

In comparison to Canada or Australia, what I would describe as a certain attenuation in identifying the continental United States as a settler colony may also be attributed to an ideology of American exceptionalism and history of empire building, which are possibly the most exemplary expressions of settler colonialism. Indeed, what distinguishes the United States as a settler colony is the way it epitomizes a paradigm of endless invasion of both Indigenous *and* foreign lands.[11] Unlike former franchise colonies, such as British India or the Dutch East Indies—regions where economic exploitation occurred *without* large-scale white settlement—settler colonies are also largely immune to decolonization because settlers don't leave. They are "breakaway" colonies insofar as they transfer the power of the metropolitan center to the periphery, *subverting* a normative logic of colonialism.[12] In establishing British settler colonies, it was specifically land acquisition that was the primary objective rather than the exploitation of Indigenous labor.[13] Because white settlement was a primary goal in British North America, Australia, New Zealand, and South Africa, the process of detaching from British imperial rule—becoming "postcolonial" as it were—did not structurally alter the colonial relationship between settlers and Indigenous populations. In other words, there is no "post" to settler colonialism. As Werner

Biermann and Reinhart Kössler reflect on the irony of revolutionary settler independence movements like those in the United States, "settler counter-imperialism cannot, in any sense, be considered of an emancipatory nature, but rather as a defense for atavistic forms of exploitation which by this token take on a politically anachronistic stature as well."[14] Therefore, in settler colonies, the diminishing role of an imperial metropole actually facilitated successive stages of Indigenous elimination that involved invasion, removal, relocation, reservation, termination, and assimilation. This renders a paradoxical situation where, as Robert J. C. Young describes it, "the postcolonial operates simultaneously as the colonial."[15]

THE TWO STATES OF SETTLER COLONIALISM

In a nation with such fraught contexts of forced migration, immigrant exclusion, relocation, and deportation, questions inevitably arise over whether non-Indigenous but racialized peoples—such as slaves, refugees, or the undocumented—are unequivocally "settlers." The responses to this question have been varied. On the one hand, Lorenzo Veracini has distinguished migrants from settlers, claiming that "migrants, by definition, move to *another* country and lead diasporic lives, settlers on the contrary, move . . . to *their* country."[16] The crucial distinction that Veracini draws turns on the question of sovereignty: settlers bring their sovereignty with them, and migrants do not. Jodi A. Byrd extends this kind of distinction by offering the term *arrivant* to "signify those people forced into the Americas through the violence of European and Anglo-American colonialism and imperialism around the globe."[17] Patrick Wolfe, on the other hand, registers unwavering opposition to any view that suggests that a lack of embodied sovereignty—or any other condition of migration—has any bearing on what he casts as an inexorable logic "whereby settler societies, for all their internal complexities, uniformly require the elimination of Native alternatives."[18] He further charges that any "post-structuralist indictment of binarism endorses colonial policymaking" because it implies that the "originary binarism has become dissolved or transcended."[19] Below I look more closely at Wolfe's argument and its implications for framing race and Indigeneity before turning to Afro-pessimist arguments regarding an essential black/nonblack binary.

Taking each of Wolfe's points in turn, my primary objective is to show how he both evacuates race and projects voluntarism into his characterization of the settler. Directing his comments primarily at U.S. academics, Wolfe's argument rests on two main points that (1) reject the relevance of migrant voluntarism as a constitutive feature of the settler and (2) decouple race from settler colonialism.[20] First, he argues that it is a mistake to define the settler according to a criterion of voluntarism because the opposition between the Native and the settler is "a structural relationship rather than an effect of the will."[21] This framework applies to enslaved people too:

> The fact that enslaved people *immigrated* against their will—to cite the most compelling case for voluntarism—does not alter the structural fact that their presence, however involuntary, was part of the process of Native dispossession. White convicts [in Australia] also came against their will. Does this mean their descendants are not settlers?[22]

While his claim that being a settler is "not an effect of the will" has merit, he implicitly preserves the voluntarism that he otherwise rejects in his construction of the slave. In particular, he draws on the Australian context in which white convict labor was imported from Britain in order to pose the rhetorical question: "does this mean their descendants are not settlers?" Given that Wolfe concedes that white convicts in Australia did not pass the condition of their criminal enslavement onto their offspring, it is surprising that he presents it as a comparative equivalent to a U.S. history of African slavery. The very content of black racialization has been based on the exclusive and transferable condition of racial enslavement. Furthermore, his repeated usage of "immigrants" projects into every migrant a set of voluntaristic assumptions and functions as a problematic stand-in for widely divergent conditions of voluntary and forced migration that are central features of the United States' specific configuration as a settler colony. Former slaves, war refugees, and undocumented migrants are no more "immigrants" than Indigenous peoples. More pointedly, from the standpoint of Afropessimism, Jared Sexton states, "No amount of tortured logic could permit the analogy to be drawn between a former slave population and an immigrant population, no matter how low-flung the latter group."[23] Wolfe's blanket usage of "immigration" also papers over a long history of racialized immigrant restriction, which barred or restricted the flow of Asian migrants from the late nineteenth century until 1965. And for those Asian migrants who remained "aliens ineligible for citizenship" until the mid-twentieth century or the Japanese civilians who were relocated as "enemy aliens" during World War II, immigrant status was inordinately conditioned by race. In the contemporary context, racialized vulnerability to deportation of undocumented, guest-worker, or other provisional migrant populations similarly exceed the conceptual boundaries that attend "the immigrant." The fact that I am pointing this out doesn't absolve any of these groups from being willing or unwitting participants in a settler colonial structure that is driven to eliminate Indigenous people. However, folding them into a generalized settler position through voluntaristic assumptions constrains our ability to understand how their racialized vulnerability and disposability supports a settler colonial project.

Wolfe's second point is to argue that settler supremacy and white supremacy, while often being "privileges that are fused and mutually compounding in social life,"[24] are actually categorically distinct modalities of power. He turns to the examples of colonized Tibetans, West Papuans, Khoi-san, Kashmiris and others to demonstrate that the terms of their colonial dispossession have nothing to do with race. He writes, "Campaigning against White supremacism would not help these people. It would be more likely to delight their colonisers."[25] In sum, one's status as a settler is neither an effect of the will nor a condition of one's racial supremacy. Being a settler is solely constituted by being structurally opposed to Indigenous peoples. Here, Wolfe misses the point while overstating his case. While white supremacy may not be a feature of the colonial dispossession of Tibetans, doesn't a Chinese supremacy exercise *racial* dominance over Tibetans? The example of the Khoisan is even more peculiar. It is not clear how this Indigenous population in South Africa is not shaped by the vestiges of apartheid and enduring structures of white supremacy given that their land and water were dispossessed by European settlers in what is now Cape Town.[26] Moreover, in Wolfe's assertion that "the primary motive [of settler colonialism] is not race . . . but access to territory," such a claim effectively evacuates the proprietorial nature of whiteness, one that led W. E. B. Du Bois to define "Whiteness [as] the ownership of the earth forever and ever, Amen."[27] Racial supremacy shifts over time and space—as do constructions of whiteness. Nevertheless, I propose that racial dynamics are internal rather than external to the logic of settler colonialism in North America.

AFRO-PESSIMISM AND THE TOTALITY

The paradigm of Afro-pessimism offers an interesting corollary to the Indigenous/settler binary discussed above. My discussion of this critical theory rests on the terms of its binary formulation and rejection of Indigenous sovereignty that have been advanced by Jared Sexton and Frank Wilderson, perhaps the most vocal proponents of this school of thought.[28]

My goal here is to respond to their critique of Indigenous sovereignty by reframing the relation between colonialism and racial slavery and to challenge the antidialectical stance of Afro-pessimist critique. Although Afro-pessimism rejects Marxian political economic analysis,[29] it operationalizes a revised paradigm of economic determinism to install instead an antiblack base that generates a global racial superstructure.

Rather than reinscribe a black/white opposition, Afro-pessimism charts a black/nonblack binary that evolves out of the history of racial slavery. The reason for absorbing whiteness into a variable condition of nonblackness is to deemphasize white power and instead emphasize the singularity and paradigmatic status of racial blackness as the essential condition of enslaveability. According to Sexton, white people are better termed "*all nonblacks . . .* because it is a racial blackness as a necessary condition for enslavement that matters most, rather than whiteness as a sufficient condition for freedom."[30] In what Sexton terms an "unequally arrayed category of nonblackness," Wilderson designates white subjects as the "senior partners" and other non-white, nonblack racialized subjects as the "junior partners of civil society."[31] The indelible, iterative structure of racial slavery is what animates our contemporary moment—what Sexton refers to as a future anterior—a mathematical terror that Saidiya Hartman grounds in the "racial calculus and a political arithmetic that were entrenched centuries ago."[32] Rejecting the Indigenous/settler opposition put forward by Wolfe, Sexton states that the U.S.-born slave-descended population "suffers the status of being neither the native nor the foreigner, neither the colonizer nor the colonized."[33] Thus blackness is both a lived impossibility and categorical exception. Wilderson further contends that black life is an evacuated historical category, a lived entity that is "*off the record.*"[34] Unlike Native Americans, whom he claims have recourse to historical modes of ontological embodiment—such that they exist "liminally as half-death and half-life between the Slave (black) and the Human (White or nonblack)"—black people are a categorical negation, part of "America's structuring irrationality" that engenders the coherence and rationality of white life.[35]

Wilderson and Sexton extend these arguments about the relationality of black and Indigenous ontologies of non- or half-life respectively to further interrogate the validity of Indigenous sovereignty movements. These arguments are taken from Wilderson's articles and 2010 monograph *Red, White & Black: Cinema and the Structure of U.S. Antagonisms,* which are expanded upon in Sexton's 2014 article, "The *Vel* of Slavery: Tracking the Figure of the Unsovereign." To begin then with Wilderson's formulation, for him Indigeneity differs from antiblackness because Indigenous sovereignty struggles engage in a politics of state recognition that is categorically unavailable to black subjects. More than this, Wilderson claims that Native sovereignty claims ultimately uphold rather than undermine white supremacy and the coherence of the U.S. nation-state. He writes, "White supremacy has made good use of the Indian subject's positionality: a positionality which fortifies and extends the interlocutory life of America as a coherent (albeit genocidal) idea, because treaties are forms of articulation, and discussions brokered between two groups presumed to possess the same kind of historical currency: sovereignty."[36] In their critical alliance, Wilderson and Sexton emphasize how "the dynamics of Negrophobia are animated . . . by a preoccupation with sovereignty."[37]

The claim of Negrophobic Indigenous sovereignty is rooted in Wilderson's somewhat selective reading of Chris Eyre's 2002 feature film *Skins* about Native American vigilantism and alcoholism. Here he argues that the Native American protagonist Rudy Yellow Lodge's preoccupation with spirituality and sovereignty animates his Negrophobia. Wilderson's rationale for this interpretation is that Rudy has the capacity to be aligned with a politics of genocide rather than sovereignty, the latter of which forecloses a shared antagonism with black existence. Such an emphasis on sovereignty therefore represents a "de-escalation of antagonism to the level of conflict."[38] In particular, Wilderson links Rudy's investment in sovereignty to his anger at two Native teens for "acting 'Black' . . . their grunting voices and aggressive body language [indicating] that they are talking 'Black.'"[39] Because the teens get into a fight with one another, Wilderson registers Rudy's "sovereign" rejection of the corrosive effects of blackness. The teens' mimicry of blackness is presented as the *cause* of their fight: "Rap lyrics, dialect, and Black male body language have pulled these two young men into a pit of absolute dereliction and cultural abandonment," which leads Wilderson to conclude that "Blackness is at the heart of Native American autogenocide."[40] As a result, as Sexton elaborates, Indigenous sovereignty can only mobilize a politics of "resurgence or recovery [that] is bound to regard the slave as 'the position of the unthought.'"[41] Slavery is incompatible with the presumptions of sovereign recuperation of and governance over land, identity, and cultures, because slavery "is not a loss that the self experiences . . . but rather the loss of any self that could experience such loss."[42] These points form the basic architecture for Sexton's ultimate claim that sovereignty should be jettisoned in favor of the more radical antagonistic project of abolition.

To begin digesting these claims, one finds a certain contradiction in the empirical relation of Indigeneity and blackness that Wilderson and Sexton present. Wilderson's suggestion that a shared genocidal antagonism would potentially form a correspondence between Indigeneity and antiblackness is somewhat at odds with Sexton's claim that racial slavery subsumes all other modalities of power. It is only through our realization of the exceptionality of antiblackness, Sexton writes, that "might help not only to break down false dichotomies, and perhaps pose a truer one, but also to reveal the ways that the study of slavery is already and of necessity the study of capitalism, colonialism, and settler colonialism, among other things."[43] Here I interpret Sexton's rejection of a Native/settler opposition as among the "false dichotomies" that should be dispensed with in order to install a black/nonblack "truer" dichotomy. However, and this is my point, Wilderson's and Sexton's divergent emphases put the empirical status of Indigeneity in flux. On the one hand, Indigenous sovereignty is conceptualized primarily as a screen: an "obscene supplement" of the settler nation-state,[44] an antiblack expression of false consciousness, or a lost opportunity to apply the motif of genocide and share in an antagonism that relates to black social death. That is, the claim that sovereignty "de-escalates" a genocidal antagonism to "conflict" suggests that a more authentic truth of Indigeneity is genocide, which means that the unrealized fact of Indigeneity *is* its empirical analogy to black social death. But on the other hand, Sexton forcefully rejects any claim to an empirically based analogy, claiming that antiblackness trumps Indigeneity just as racial slavery trumps settler colonialism. And so the potential relations that Wilderson sets up through a critique of sovereignty are at best irrelevant or at worse false in Sexton's absolute claim that slavery stands alone as the "threshold of the political world."[45] I suggest that this wavering relation/nonrelation of antiblackness and Indigeneity exhibited in Wilderson's and Sexton's work reveal the problem in any totalizing approach to the heterogeneous constitution of racial difference in settler colonies.

Beyond this inconsistency, the liberal multiculturalist agenda that Wilderson and Sexton project into Indigenous sovereignty willfully evacuates any Indigenous *refusal* of a colonial politics of recognition. Among other broad strokes, Sexton states, "as a rule, Native Studies reproduces the dominant liberal political narrative of emancipation and enfranchisement."[46] This provides a basis for Wilderson's assertion that Indigenous sovereignty engages in a liberal politics of state legitimation through recognition because "treaties are forms of articulation" that buttress "the interlocutory life of America as a coherent (albeit genocidal) idea."[47] But such a depoliticized liberal project is frankly incompatible with Indigenous activism and scholarship that emerges from Native studies in North America. The main

argument in Glen Sean Coulthard's book *Red Skin, White Masks* is to categorically reject "the liberal recognition-based approach to Indigenous self-
determination."[48] This is not a politics of legitimizing Indigenous nations
through state recognition but rather one of refusal, a refusal to be recognized and thus interpellated by the settler colonial nation-state. Drawing
on Fanon, Coulthard describes the "necessity on the part of the oppressed
to 'turn away' from their other-oriented master-dependency, and to instead
struggle for freedom on their own terms and in accordance with their own
values."[49] It is also difficult to reconcile the depoliticized narrative of "resurgence and recovery" that Wilderson and Sexton attribute to Indigenous
sovereignty in the face of Idle No More, the anticapitalist Indigenous sovereignty movement in Canada whose national railway and highway blockades
have seriously destabilized the expropriation of natural resources for the
global market. These are examples that Coulthard describes as "direct action"
rather than negotiation—in other words, *antagonism,* not conflict resolution:

> They [blockades] are a crucial act of negation insofar as they seek to impede
> or block the flow of resources currently being transported to international
> markets from oil and gas fields, refineries, lumber mills, mining operations,
> and hydroelectric facilities located on the dispossessed lands of Indigenous
> nations. These modes of direct action . . . seek to have a negative impact on
> the economic infrastructure that is core to the colonial accumulation of
> capital in settler-political economies like Canada's.[50]

These tactics are part of what Audra Simpson calls a "cartography of refusal"
that "negates the authority of the other's gaze."[51] It is impossible to frame
the blockade movement, which has become the greatest threat to Canada's
resource agenda,[52] as a struggle for "enfranchisement." Idle No More is not
in "conflict" with the Canadian nation-state; it is in a struggle against the
very premise of settler colonial capitalism that requires the elimination of
Indigenous peoples. As Coulthard states unambiguously, "For Indigenous
nations to live, capitalism must die."[53]

But perhaps my own defense of Indigenous decolonization movements
for sovereignty begs a larger question about whether sovereignty in itself
offers a radical politics that can encompass or mobilize a black radical tradition rooted in the project of abolition. And it is here that I agree with Sexton's
intervention to problematize the idea that antiracist agendas must emerge
from the foundational priority of Indigenous sovereignty and restoration of
land.[54] But against the totalizing frame of Afro-pessimism, I want to stress

instead the pitfalls of any antidialectical approach to the political economy of the settler colonial racial state from the position of *either* Indigenous or antiblack exceptionalism. Settler colonial racial capitalism is not a thing but a social relation. As such, it is not produced out of the *causal* relationships that Sexton puts forward here: "Slavery, as it were, precedes and prepares the way for colonialism, its forebear or fundament or support. Colonialism, as it were, the issue or heir of slavery, its outgrowth or edifice or monument."[55] The nearly totalizing black existential frame is similarly based on a questionable construction of epistemic privilege:

> [black existence] does relate to the totality; it indicates the (repressed) truth of the political and economic system. That is to say, the whole range of positions within the racial formation is most fully understood from this vantage point, not unlike the way in which the range of gender and sexual variance under patriarchal and heteronormative regimes is most fully understood through lenses that are feminist and queer.[56]

According to Sexton, no other oppression is reducible to antiblackness, but the relative totality of antiblackness is the privileged perspective from which to understand racial formation more broadly. But unlike the way feminist and queer critical theory interrogate heteropatriarchy from a subjectless standpoint, Sexton's entire point seems to rest on the very specificity and singularity—rather than subjectlessness—of black critical theory's capacity to understand race. The privilege of this embodied viewpoint similarly relies on rigidly binaristic conceptions of land and bodily integrity. He writes, "If the indigenous relation to land precedes and exceeds any regime of property, then the slave's inhabitation of the earth precedes and exceeds any prior relation to land—landlessness. And selflessness is the correlate. No ground for identity, no ground to stand (on)."[57] In other words, the slave's nonrelation to her body precedes and exceeds any other body's relation to land. However, the settler colonial designation of the United States and Canada as *terra nullius*—as legally empty lands—denies the very corporeality of Indigenous populations to inhabit land, much less have any rights to it. Alongside genocidal elimination, the erasure of Indigenous corporeal existence is inseparable from the ground it doesn't stand on, or is removed from.

For the same reason that the economic reductionism of orthodox Marxism has been discredited, such an argument that frames racial slavery as a base for a colonial superstructure similarly fails to take into account the dialectics of settler colonial capitalism. The political economy of settler colonial capitalism is more appropriately figured as an ecology of power relations than a linear chain of events. Relinquishing any conceptual privilege that might be attributed to Indigeneity, alternatively, Coulthard offers a useful anti-exceptionalist stance: "the colonial relation should not be understood as a primary locus of 'base' from which these other forms of oppression flow, but rather as the inherited background field within which market, racist, patriarchal, and state relations *converge*."[58] From this view, race and colonialism form the matrix of the settler colonial racial state.

Putting colonial land and enslaved labor at the center of a dialectical analysis, we can see that blackness is neither reducible to Indigenous land nor Indigeneity to enslaved labor. Indigenous peoples and slaves are not reducible to each other because settler colonialism abides by a dual logic that is originally driven to eliminate Native peoples from land and mix the land with enslaved black labor. If land is the basis of settler colonialists' relationship to Indigenous peoples, it is labor that frames that relationship with enslaved peoples. We can draw on Patrick Wolfe's important points about the heterogeneous racial effects of such a settler formation based on Indigenous land and enslaved labor. To summarize those points, the *racial* content of Indigenous peoples is the mirror opposite of blackness. From the beginning, an eliminatory project was driven to reduce Native populations through genocidal wars and later through statistical elimination through blood quantum and assimilationist policies. For slaves, an opposite logic of exclusion was driven to *increase*, not eliminate, the population of slaves. One logic does not cause the other; rather, they work together to serve a unitary end in increasing white settler property in the form of land and an enslaved labor force. As a result, in the postemancipation, postfrontier era, the racial content of Indigenous peoples is entirely dissolvable and eradicable. Alternatively, the racial content of blackness remains absolute and essential, and maintains an infinite capacity to contaminate. As Wolfe states, "the respective racializations . . . were diametrically opposed, in a manner that reflected and preserved the foundational distinction between land and labor. For whereas race for black people became an indelible trait that would survive any amount of admixture, race for Indians became an inherently descending quantity that was terminally susceptible to dilution."[59] One consequence is that the phrase "separate but equal" can take two meanings: as either an injurious legal relic or a sovereign politics of the future.[60] Given this stark distinction in racial ontologies, any critical theory that views race and colonialism as a causal rather than dialectical relation is incapable of exposing these inextricable logics of settler colonialism.

PRIMITIVE ACCUMULATION AND ITS IRRATIONALITY

In order to recuperate the frame of political economy, a focus on the dialectic of racial slavery and settler colonialism leads to important revisions of Karl Marx's theory of primitive accumulation. In particular, Marx designates the transition from feudal to capitalist social relations as a violent process of primitive accumulation whereby "conquest, enslavement, robbery, murder, in short, force, play the greatest part."[61] For Marx, this results in the expropriation of the worker, the proletariat, who becomes the privileged subject of capitalist revolution. If we consider primitive accumulation as a persistent structure rather than event, both Afro-pessimism and settler colonial studies destabilize normative conceptions of capitalism through the conceptual displacements of the proletariat. As Coulthard demonstrates, in considering Indigenous peoples in relation to primitive accumulation, "it appears that the history and experience of *dispossession,* not proletarianization, has been the dominant background structure shaping the character of the historical relationship between Indigenous peoples and the Canadian state."[62] It is thus dispossession of land through genocidal elimination, relocation, and theft that animates Indigenous resistance and anticapitalism and "less around our emergent status as 'rightless proletarians.'"[63] If we extend the frame of primitive accumulation to the question of slavery, it is the dispossession of the slave's body rather than the proletarianization of labor that both precedes and exceeds the frame of settler colonial and global modernity.

On this point Afro-pessimism offers a unique and incisive formulation of black labor. Dispensing with a view that slavery was a labor system— including Andrea Smith's assessment that "African Americans have been traditionally *valued* for their labor"[64]—Sexton and Wilderson decouple slavery from a normative conception of labor. The slave, in their estimation, is a figure of anti-labor who calls into question the very legitimacy of productive work.[65] Rather than a labor system, slavery represented foremost a capitalist property system that was kick-started by the "'accumulation' of black bodies regardless of their utility as laborers."[66] Thus the slave cannot be thought of as a worker, because the "slave makes a demand which is in excess of the demand made by the worker."[67] That is to say, while the worker demands fairness and improved labor conditions the slave demands that all production cease regardless of its democratization because "work is not an organic principle for the slave."[68] This argument is fueled by Wilderson's and Sexton's general critique of Marxism, whose central tenets fall apart, they argue, in the presence of the black body. Here I quote Wilderson's delineation of the unrecognized but generative condition of blackness for initiating capitalist modernity and later resolving crises of capitalism:

> The absence of black subjectivity from the crux of Marxist discourse is symptomatic of the discourse's inability to cope with the possibility that the generative subject of capitalism, the black body of the fifteenth and sixteenth centuries, and the generative subject that resolves late-capital's over-accumulation crisis, the black (incarcerated) body of the twentieth and twenty-first centuries, do not reify the basic categories which structure Marxist conflict: the categories of work, production, exploitation, historical self-awareness, and above all, hegemony.[69]

Because antiblackness is a terror formation rather than a hegemonic one, overthrowing capitalism cannot guarantee emancipation. There are no demands that the exploited worker can put forward that can satisfy or solve the experience of black social death, which prohibits the slave from entering into a transaction of value. Moreover, Steve Martinot and Jared Sexton dispel the assumption that "if racism can be made not useful to the relations of production or the security of territorial boundaries, it will fade away from the social landscape like the proverbial withering away of the state."[70] In their estimation, the precarity and irrationality of blackness operate outside the normative and rational circuits of capitalism. Carrying this logic forward into the neoliberal age, as Tamara Nopper clarifies, "as workers, African Americans are treated as possessing no productive value and contributing to no economy or nation."[71] The social death of the black body is thus an irrational and despotic foundation on which the structuring rationality of American civil society and capitalism are based and enabled.

While I question the notion that slavery does not function as a labor system, Wilderson makes an important point that the slave exceeds a normative Marxian conception of the productive worker. Adding to the black subject's exclusion from this category of worker, I would argue that Indigenous peoples in settler colonies are similarly constituted outside of a hegemonic labor paradigm. To support this, we can turn to Wilderson's own example of the Khoisan of South Africa. He argues that when European anthropologists encountered the Khoisan they were deemed "without character" because they did not work.[72] This perceived idleness was therefore grounds for their annihilation. As Wilderson recounts, this idleness had been "a) counterposed to work and b) criminalized and designated with the status of sin."[73] While the Khoisan animate the larger incoherence of a global antiblackness, they are also an Indigenous population subject to the eliminatory logics of settler colonialism. In many ways, their experience parallels that of Native Americans, whose lands were dispossessed on the basis of their presumed failure to work; that is, their so-called failure to cultivate land or enclose it. This colonial logic was derived from John Locke's *Two Treatises of Government,* which argued that Indigenous peoples had "no inherent right to property in land and that only appropriation through labor provided the rights of ownership."[74] A colonial construction of work (or absence of) was thus the justification for British settlers to claim property rights through agricultural labor and enclosed settlement. These points relate to an overall logic of settler colonialism that Wolfe lays out, insofar as "settler colonialism seeks to *replace the native* on their land rather than extract surplus value by mixing their labor with a colony's natural resources."[75] The racial logic that evacuates the humanity of the Khoisan works in tandem with a settler colonial logic driven to replace Indigenous peoples by eliminating them—rather than by exploiting their labor. For Indigenous populations in North America, moreover, there are similarly no demands that the exploited worker can put forward to solve the experience of Indigenous elimination and dispossession. The Indigenous body's metaphoric distance from labor also stands as an irrational outside to settler colonial political economy. This opens up a view of how the internal dialectics of the racial state shape and distort the view of social labor, revealing irrationalities that exceed normative circuits of capitalism.

Expanding the scope beyond a black/Indigenous frame, we can explore how other groups have been subject to or have expressed different forms of economic irrationality in the context of settler colonialism. For example, since the nineteenth century, the content of Asian racialization has often turned on an *excessive* efficiency responsible for the destruction of normative proletariat labor. Here too the Asian laborer's negative relation to the extraction of surplus value frustrates a presumption of capitalism's rationality. In the nineteenth-century context of Chinese railroad building in North America, the connection between the Chinese and the abstract domination of capitalism evolved through their identification with a mode of efficiency that was aligned with a perverse temporality of domestic and social reproduction. In many ways, the Chinese became the personification of Marx's formulation of "abstract labor." Here abstract labor, which represents a social average of labor time to produce a use-value in order to express its quantitative value during exchange, is set into opposition with concrete labor, the actual time and place of a specific laboring activity that expresses its qualitative use-value. Through the symbolic alignment of Chinese bodies with perverse forms of accelerated temporality, their human labor was rendered disembodied, abstract. White bodies, on the other hand, were symbolically associated with concrete labor, which establishes a commodity's quality. In other words, the Chinese personified the quantitative sphere of abstract labor, which threatened the concrete, qualitative sphere of white labor's social reproduction.

Whiteness, too, has distorted its relation to capitalist modernity at key moments in history by invoking an ideology of romantic anticapitalism. Enduring features of Romanticism, the aesthetic movement that emerged in the nineteenth century, exhibit such a biologized worldview in its human (and often racial and national) identification with the purity of the natural world, portrayed as the valorized antithesis to the negative influences of urbanization and industrialization. From the antimaterialism expressed in Henry David Thoreau's excursion to Walden Pond in the nineteenth century to Christopher McCandless's 1992 divestment of all symbols of material wealth—even setting fire to his remaining cash—for a life in the wilderness, we can discern a romantic attachment to a pure and revitalizing construction of nature, in contrast to the alienation attributed to capitalist modernity. Nature therefore personifies concrete, perfected human relations against the social degeneration caused by the abstract circuits of capitalism. This is a mode of white settler identification that Shari M. Huhndorf calls "going Native," which functions to cover over colonial invasion and reimagine a natural affiliation to the land.[76] Within this ideology of settler colonial belonging, who else but the Native, whose alignment with a state of nature is perceived to be wholly removed from the sphere of capitalism, represents the idealized figure of this symbolic pursuit? Who else but the enslaved black subject remains as the reviled antithesis of that anticapitalism, as the originary object of modernity? The purpose of these brief examples is to suggest that an ongoing settler colonial structure of primitive accumulation and ideology of romantic anticapitalism require that we imagine far different demands than those that emerge from Marx's beleaguered proletariat.

By way of conclusion, I want to question the impetus for an Afro-pessimist or any other attempt to dismantle the validity of settler colonial critique by recourse to the issue of Native sovereignty.[77] While my argument in this essay has been to problematize the notion that settler colonial racial capitalism is a zero sum game, I think it is also important to acknowledge a longer institutional context that has historically sidelined Indigenous cultural politics in order to prioritize systems of oppression that target other gendered and racialized populations. Indeed, Indigenous struggles have often exceeded the dominant conceptual paradigms of U.S. ethnic studies anchored by race, citizenship, war and labor migration, and transnationalism and diaspora, to name only a few. Despite the crucial importance of these frameworks in the institutional history of ethnic studies, they have tended to relegate Indigeneity rather than blackness to the "position of the unthought." My hope is that a *critical* ethnic studies frame will enable a durable Native American critical existence in relation to the totality. Being, not nothingness.

IYKO DAY is associate professor of English at Mount Holyoke College and author of *Alien Capital: Asian Racialization and the Logic of Settler Colonial Capitalism* (2016).

NOTES

I am indebted to Danika Medak-Saltzman, Tony Tiongson, Sylvia Chan-Malik, Jodi Kim, David Hernández, and Dory Nason for valuable conversations and generous feedback.

1. Jared Sexton, "People-of-Color-Blindness: Notes on the Afterlife of Slavery," *Social Text* 28, no. 2 (2010): 48.

2. Patrick Wolfe, "Recuperating Binarism: A Heretical Introduction," *Settler Colonial Studies* 3, nos. 3–4 (2013): 257, 258.

3. Frank B. Wilderson III, "Gramsci's Black Marx: Whither the Slave in Civil Society," *Social Identities* 9, no. 2 (2003): 238.

4. Jared Sexton, "The *Vel* of Slavery: Tracking the Figure of the Unsovereign," *Critical Sociology* (December 2014): 2.

5. See, for example, Laura Pulido and David Lloyd, "In the Long Shadow of the Settler: On Israeli and U.S. Colonialisms," *American Quarterly* 62, no. 4 (2010); Rosaura Sánchez and Beatrice Pita, "Rethinking Settler Colonialism," *American Quarterly* 66, no. 4 (2014); Candace Fujikane and Jonathan Y. Okamura, eds., *Asian Settler Colonialism: From Local Governance to the Habits of Everyday Life in Hawai'i* (Honolulu: University of Hawai'i Press, 2008).

6. Saidiya Hartman, *Lose Your Mother: A Journal along the Atlantic Slave Route* (New York: Farrar, Straus and Giroux, 2007), 45.

7. Bill V. Mullen, "Global Intifada," *Counterpunch*, November 27, 2012, http://www.counterpunch.org/2012/11/27/global-intifada/.

8. Fujikane and Okamura, *Asian Settler Colonialism*.

9. Dean Saranillio, "Why Asian Settler Colonialism Matters," *Settler Colonial Studies* 2, nos. 3–4 (2013): 286.

10. Patrick Wolfe, *Settler Colonialism and the Transformation of Anthropology: The Politics and Poetics of an Ethnographic Event* (London: Cassell, 1999), 2.

11. There is a long list of present-day (non-post) colonies, dependent, trust and unincorporated territories, overseas departments, and other colonial entities that include British Gibraltar, the Falklands/Malvinas; Danish Greenland; Dutch Antilles; French Guiana, Martinique, Réunion, St. Pierre, and Miquelon; U.S. Puerto Rico, Samoa, and Virgin Islands; Spanish Ceuta, Melilla, and the Canary Islands. See Robert J. C. Young, *Postcolonialism: An Historical Introduction* (Oxford: Blackwell, 2001), 3.

12. Anne McClintock, "The Angel of Progress: Pitfalls of the Term 'Post-Colonialism,'" *Social Text*, no. 31–32 (1992): 84–98.

13. Patrick Wolfe, "Land, Labor, and Difference: Elementary Structures of Race," *The American Historical Review* 106, no. 3 (2001): 866–905.

14. Werner Biermann and Reinhart Kössler, "The Settler Mode of Production: The Rhodesian Case," *Review of African Political Economy*, no. 18 (May–August 1980): 115.

15. Young, *Postcolonialism*, 20.

16. Lorenzo Veracini, *Settler Colonialism: A Theoretical Overview* (London: Palgrave Macmillan, 2010), 3.

17. Jodi A. Byrd, *The Transit of Empire: Indigenous Critiques of Colonialism* (Minneapolis: University of Minnesota Press, 2011), xix.

18. Wolfe, "Recuperating Binarism," 257.

19. Ibid., 259, 257.

20. Ibid., 257.

21. Ibid., 263.

22. Ibid. (emphasis mine).

23. Jared Sexton, "The Social Life of Social Death: On Afro-Pessimism and Black Optimism," *InTensions Journal*, no. 5 (Fall/Winter 2011): 18.

24. Wolfe, "Recuperating Binarism," 264.

25. Ibid.

26. See Mohamed Adhikari, *Not White Enough, Not Black Enough: Racial Identity in the South African Coloured Community* (Athens: Ohio University Press, 2005).

27. Patrick Wolfe, "Settler-Colonialism and the Elimination of the Native," *Journal of Genocide Studies* 8, no. 4 (2006): 388; W. E. B. Du Bois, quoted in Marilyn Lake and Henry Reynolds, *Drawing the Global Colour Line: White Men's Countries and the International Challenge of Racial Equality* (Cambridge: Cambridge University Press, 2008), 2.

28. Scholars referenced in connection to Afro-pessimism include Hortense Spillers, Saidiya Hartman, David Marriott, Franz Fanon, and Orlando Patterson. See Fred Moten's engagement with black optimism and pessimism in "Blackness and Nothingness (Mysticism in the Flesh)," *South Atlantic Quarterly* 112, no. 4 (2013): 737–81.

29. See Wilderson, "Gramsci's Black Marx."

30. Sexton, "People-of-Color-Blindness," 36.

31. Frank B. Wilderson III, *Red, White & Black: Cinema and the Structure of U.S. Antagonisms* (Durham, N.C.: Duke University Press, 2010), 38.

32. Hartman, *Lose Your Mother*, 7, quoted in Sexton, "The Social Life of Social Death," 19.

33. Sexton, "People-of-Color-Blindness," 41.

34. Wilderson, "Gramsci's Black Marx," 236.

35. Wilderson, *Red, White & Black*, 23, 231. For the first category, Rights or Entitlements, Wilderson notes that "here even Native Americans provide categories for the record when one thinks of how the Iroquois constitution, for example, becomes the American constitution." The second category is Sovereignty, which inheres in those people, including Native Americans, whose sovereignty was "taken by force and dint of broken treaties" and which can have a future history insofar as numerous Native American tribes have submitted applications for federal recognition. The third is Immigration, whereby "contestations over the legitimacy of arrival, immigration, or of sovereignty" is a category of subjecthood for either white or racialized migrants. But the African American does not generate historical categories, according to Wilderson, hence the anomalous nonbeing of black exception.

36. Wilderson, "Gramsci's Black Marx," 236.

37. Sexton, "The *Vel* of Slavery," 10

38. Ibid.

39. Wilderson, *Red, White & Black*, 227.

40. Ibid., 227, 228. Wilderson acknowledges that "someone watching this scene in a theater would have comprehended none of this." Ibid., 227.

41. Sexton, "The *Vel* of Slavery," 9, quoting Wilderson and Hartman.

42. Ibid.

43. Ibid., 11.

44. Slavoj Žižek adapts Jacques Derrida's notion of the supplement as something that, in giving coherence to the dominant term in a binary, subverts the logic of that binary. For Žižek, the obscene supplement *reinforces* rather than destabilizes the political system. See Slavoj Žižek, *The Plague of Fantasies* (New York: Verso, 1997), 28–51.

45. Sexton, "The *Vel* of Slavery," 11.

46. Ibid., 12n10.

47. Wilderson, "Gramsci's Black Marx," 236, quoted in Sexton, "The *Vel* of Slavery," 10.

48. Glen Sean Coulthard, *Red Skin, White Masks: Rejecting the Colonial Politics of Recognition* (Minneapolis: University of Minnesota Press, 2014), 23.

49. Ibid., 43.

50. Ibid., 170.

51. Audra Simpson, *Mohawk Interruptus: Political Life across the Borders of Settler States* (Durham, N.C.: Duke University Press, 2014), 33, 24.

52. Martin Lukacs and Shiri Pasternak, "Aboriginal Rights a Threat to Canada's Resource Agenda," *The Guardian*, March 14, 2014.

53. Coulthard, *Red Skin, White Masks*, 173.

54. Sexton, "The *Vel* of Slavery," 5.

55. Ibid., 11.

56. Sexton, "People-of-Color-Blindness," 48.

57. Sexton, "The *Vel* of Slavery," 11.

58. Coulthard, *Red Skin, White Masks*, 14.

59. Wolfe, "Land, Labor, and Difference," 887.

60. I am thinking in particular of Indigenous mobilizing in Canada around the "White Paper," which would have terminated Indigenous populations' special status.

61. Karl Marx, *Capital, Volume I*, trans. Ben Fowkes (London: Penguin Books, 1990), 874.

62. Coulthard, *Red Skin, White Masks*, 13.

63. Ibid.

64. Andrea Smith, "Heteropatriarchy and the Three Pillars of White Supremacy: Rethinking Women of Color Organizing," in *The Color of Violence: The INCITE! Anthology*, ed. INCITE! Women of Color Against Violence (Boston: South End Press, 2006), 71 (emphasis mine).

65. See Tamara Nopper, "The Wages of Non-blackness: Contemporary Immigrant Rights and Discourses of Character, Productivity, and Value," *InTensions Journal*, no. 5 (2011): 1–25.

66. Wilderson, "Gramsci's Black Marx," 229.

67. Ibid., 230.

68. Ibid.

69. Ibid.

70. Steve Martinot and Jared Sexton, "The Avant-Garde of White Supremacy," *Social Identities* 9, no. 2 (2003): 178.

71. Nopper, "The Wages of Non-blackness," 19.

72. Wilderson, "Gramsci's Black Marx," 234.

73. Ibid., 235.

74. Alyosha Goldstein, "Where the Nation Takes Place: Proprietary Regimes, Antistatism, and U.S. Settler Colonialism," *South Atlantic Quarterly* 107, no. 4 (2008): 839.

75. Wolfe, "Land, Labor, and Difference," 868 (emphasis mine). See also Coulthard's more local examples of Native labor in the Canadian context in *Red Skin, White Masks*.

76. Shari M. Huhndorf, *Going Native: Indians in the American Cultural Imagination* (Ithaca, N.Y.: Cornell University Press, 2001).

77. See the discussion of critiques of Asian settler colonialism in Saranillio, "Why Asian Settler Colonialism Matters."

NEW FROM

A Shadow over Palestine
The Imperial Life of Race in America
Keith P. Feldman

How Israel and Palestine shaped the post-World War II politics of race in the United States

$24.95 hardcover | 328 pages

Physics of Blackness
Beyond the Middle Passage Epistemology
Michelle M. Wright

Reveals how assumptions we make about time and space inhibit more inclusive definitions of Blackness

$25.00 paper | $87.50 cloth | 216 pages

The White Possessive
Property, Power, and Indigenous Sovereignty
Aileen Moreton-Robinson

How whiteness operationalizes race to colonize and displace Indigenous sovereignty

$27.00 paper | $94.50 cloth | 264 pages
Indigenous Americas Series

The Poitier Effect
Racial Melodrama and Fantasies of Reconciliation
Sharon Willis

Sidney Poitier as an icon of the civil rights era, signifying racial reconciliation without threat to the white status quo

$22.50 paper | $79.00 cloth | 272 pages

Slaves of the State
Black Incarceration from the Chain Gang to the Penitentiary
Dennis Childs

A sweeping cultural history of U.S. prison slavery

$22.50 paper | $79.00 cloth | 272 pages

HIV Exceptionalism
Development through Disease in Sierra Leone
Adia Benton

Have HIV/AIDS-focused development programs ignored wider health crises in Africa?

$22.50 paper | $79.00 cloth | 192 pages
A Quadrant Book

Last Project Standing
Civics and Sympathy in Post-Welfare Chicago
Catherine Fennell

How the aftermath of public housing became an education in the rights and duties of belonging to the city

$27.00 paper | $94.50 cloth | 320 pages
A Quadrant Book | Available November 2015

Martin Heidegger Saved My Life
Grant Farred

Could there be a bigger paradox than the black man using Martin Heidegger to repel the white woman's racism?

$7.95 paper | $4.95 ebook | 102 pages
Forerunners: Ideas First Series